'Tom Allen is one of the funniest comedians in the UK, the best dressed man I know and now it turns out he is a superb writer. I hate him.' Josh Widdicombe

'Wonderfully funny, utterly charming and sharp as all Hell. Just like the man himself.' Sarah Millican

'This hilarious and touching autobiography is like a turbo charged episode of *Terry and June*. (Google it young ~ople) . . . a delightful, touching side-splitter.' Jo Brand

'An absolute joy! Funny, witty and totally charming. ou'll love him even more after reading this.' Alan Carr

Tom's rich and unique comic voice bounces off the page autifully.' Matt Lucas

his book is brilliant, funny and thoughtful just like m. I loved it'' ~i Ruffell

graphy that is sharp, tender – and of course, *Attitude*

TOM ALLEN's unique style of sharp, acerbic wit and camp, riotous storytelling has seen him become a household name in the UK. He is the host of *The Apprentice: You're Fired*, co-host of *Bake Off: The Professionals*, a regular on *Bake Off: An Extra Slice* and *There's Something About Movies*, as well as making numerous appearances on *Mock The Week*, *Live At The Apollo*, *Hypothetical*, *The Royal Variety Performance*, *8 Out Of 10 Cats*, *Cats Does Countdown*, *Would I Lie to You* and *Roast Battle*. He has also presented the flagship BBC fundraiser events *Children in Need* and *Sport Relief*.

He has his own BBC Radio 4 *Tom Allen Is Actually Not Very Nice* and appears on *Just a Minute, the News Quiz* and is a regular co-host of *Loose Ends*.

His sell out tour concluded with an unforgettable show at his spiritual home, The London Palladium, which was filmed for Channel 4. He has toured Australia which saw him nominated for Most Outstanding Show at the Melbourne International Comedy Festival.

No Shame

TOM ALLEN

HODDER studio

First published in Great Britain in 2020 by Hodder Studio
An Hachette UK company

This paperback edition published in 2021

1

A CIP catalogue record for this title is available from the British Library

Hardback ISBN 9781529348903
Trade Paperback ISBN 9781529348910
Paperback ISBN 9781529348941
eBook ISBN 9781529348927

Typeset in Bembo MT by Hewer Text UK Ltd, Edinburgh
Printed and bound in Great Britain by Clays Ltd, Elcograf S.p.A.

Hodder & Stoughton policy is to use papers that are natural, renewable
and recyclable products and made from wood grown in sustainable
forests. The logging and manufacturing processes are expected to
conform to the environmental regulations of the country of origin.

Hodder & Stoughton Ltd
Carmelite House
50 Victoria Embankment
London EC4Y 0DZ

www.hodder-studio.co.uk

For Mum and Dad, who have been kind enough
to let me stay for probably too long.

Introduction

August 2020

My dear reader,

I hope this finds you well and that you've recovered from that thing you had.

Thank you for picking up my book. I have called it *No Shame* because, when writing this book, I realised that the times in my life that I wanted to share with you all seemed to have 'shame' as a theme – largely that I have always wanted to be exuberant in some, often irritating, way but somehow felt strangled by a sense of humiliation. I've come to realise everything I have done is either a response to this feeling or a protest against it. The feeling of not having confidence in ourselves, or of feeling guilty even though we haven't done anything wrong, is, I think, something we all experience, and so I thought if I wrote about it other people might feel less alone.

When I was very young, I was shameless. For example, I remember being taken to Waitrose as a small child and deliberately getting lost – handing myself into the information desk because I knew they'd have to announce my name over the tannoy to the whole supermarket. 'Would the parent of

Thomas Allen please come to the information desk? We have him here.' In a sense, I've been lost in Waitrose ever since.

I have always been chatty. When I was around three or four years old, we went on holiday to Gran Canaria, and I'd casually leave my parents and go off and talk to the other adults, specifically older ladies staying in the resort. I always had what my mother referred to as 'a nice speaking voice' and so these older ladies would happily chat to me about everything. Tiny and perched on a sun lounger, I would get to hear about their last husband and the settlement of their divorce, the fact that they got to keep all the jewellery and how they wore it all, every day, as it shimmered and shone in the bright afternoon sun.

It was on this trip to Gran Canaria that I got lost because my dad suggested a fun game where he and Mum would take my baby brother in his pushchair down one path to the beach and I would race them on the other path. I got halfway down and got scared, so turned back. Then I wasn't sure which path they had taken and became so hopelessly lost that I knew they wouldn't be able to find me. I thought maybe I'd never see them again. I stood at the top of the paths and screened passing families for one that seemed, first, safe to ask for help, and, second, wealthy enough to provide me with a standard of living that I would be happy with if they kidnapped me or if we never found my parents again.

My mum and dad began a desperately fraught search of the beach and all the paths, with local waiters and holidaymakers enlisted to help, before the beach bar finally telephoned the hotel. 'Yes, Mrs Allen, your son is here. He is currently perched at the bar with a Coca-Cola and some crisps waving at people'. I was always confident that I could look after myself.

The realisation that I didn't fit in and that something was different about me crept in through the back door, so to speak, and got its feet under the table while I was at primary school and got even stronger as I got older. Secondary school intensified this, as I sensed that I was different to my peers and didn't seem to be fitting into any of the boxes that were set out for me. This feeling took time to overcome and for my confidence to grow, but grow it did.

Not that the journey has been straightforward or linear. Once I had the confidence to finally come out and start dating, I would often find I didn't fit in with other gay people or that I was still dealing with homophobia in its myriad forms. Sometimes, it was overt homophobia – as happened when I was on a date with a young man, and we were holding hands, and then, from a passing car, some men shouted out at us, 'Get a job!' before speeding off. We were both stunned and recoiled from each other like scolded children before we realised that they had no right to make us feel like that. What's more, what they had shouted hadn't made any sense – we both had jobs, and who goes driving around telling people to make sure they're earning a living? If anything, in my experience, gay people are very diligent high achievers and always very hard-working.

It led me to imagine that maybe bored one evening, the Doritos and dips supply exhausted, they decided to jump in the car and go for a 'Hate Drive', where they shouted out any number of insults at people. Perhaps one of their group was inexperienced in such pursuits but got overconfident and wanted to join in and ended up shouting out the first insult which came to his head. 'Get a job!'

'Garyyyyy!' his friends must have sputtered at him – 'What were you thinking?! That's the wrong type of hate for this marginalised section of society! That's an insult for people in a lower socioeconomic group than us who have struggled to find fulfilling employment in the labour market!' Poor Gary, I doubt he ever got invited on a Hate Drive again.

I have found that if we can laugh about these incidents, they lose their power over us and we manage to keep our dignity and self-esteem intact.

Shame can manifest for lots of reasons, whether it's to do with sexuality, class, money – most commonly it seems, things we have little control over. I wanted to acknowledge the moments where I have felt this and how it has motivated me to behave in a certain way or do a certain thing, however odd or eccentric it might be. Hopefully, I have also acknowledged the wonderful people I've met along the way who, often indirectly, have guided me and countered those negative feelings by being a positive presence themselves. I hope that maybe, through this book, I might endeavour to do the same for you.

I have changed some details to disguise the identities of people who are entitled to decide for themselves what does and does not shame them. There's truth in every story, but some have an extra sprinkle of icing sugar added. It's my very own confection – I hope you enjoy.

Thanks again for reading it.

Yours ever,

Tom

I

Swimming

My name is Tom Allen and I have always been forty-six years old. Since I can remember, in my head, I have always had the sense that I was an adult, and any childish encounter – from being made to sit at the children's table at a wedding to being forced to do PE at school – felt like a hideous misdemeanour and, really, is there a manager I could speak to about this?

I was born (and not delivered by angels) in June 1983 in the London suburb of Bromley. I was twelve days late and have been late ever since.

Bromley is a difficult place to describe because it doesn't really have an identity. People live there to be anonymous, comfortable and, most importantly, quiet.

Put another way, as a child did you ever get a hot feeling of shame when you started telling a story from the back of the car while your dad listened to the football results on the radio and suddenly got told mid-sentence to 'Shhhh!'? If that feeling was distilled into a geographical place that place would be Bromley. It sits proudly on the border between the grittier inner-city suburbs and the genteel 'Garden of England' itself, Kent, where aspirational baby boomers moved in the economic upswings post-1945. A Tory 'safe seat', and, as such, sometimes fearful of the wider world. It is also the location of one of the first Pizza Express restaurants outside of London.

It is a place where I continue to live now, in my parents' house, with my parents – so any condescension on my part should be taken with a pinch of salt – and it is still very much home. Bromley is a seemingly safe place, perfect for raising children, and my parents stretched themselves financially to afford a house there to bring up their two sons – my younger brother and I. Perhaps beyond what they could afford – our 1960s end-of-terrace family house is, as my dad says, '*near* the nice houses'.

It was certainly beyond what my grandparents – on my mother's side in a council flat in Sydenham, and my father's side in one room in Penge – would ever have dreamed of. Unlike lots of people in Bromley who could pay people to do their expensive renovations, my parents did all the work on the house themselves. Dad is highly skilled in all aspects of building work and can turn his hand to pretty much anything, though when he will pass on these skills to me remains to be seen. My job has largely been to stand on the sidelines and criticise, which must have been endearing for them as I suggested things like, 'Have you thought about a breakfast nook?' unsurprisingly met with, 'Have you thought about getting your own effing house?'

Bromley is a place that struggles to celebrate. For example, when it tried to pay tribute to its most famous son, David Bowie (though Brixton claims him because he was born there, it was, in truth, the sedate boredom of growing up in Bromley that gave life to Ziggy Stardust), they put a portrait of him opposite the public toilets next to Boots the Chemists. Brixton had a huge wall mural of him, and people came from all over the world to lay flowers after his passing. In Bromley they eventually put a lightning bolt mural in the pavement as a celebration of his infamous make-up, but immediately it was rebuked because it could 'confuse the blind!' or 'trip up the elderly!' Bromley certainly doesn't like spectacle, and the town's crest, which can be seen sat proudly on top of the mayor's Rolls-Royce, could read: 'Please, Don't Be Silly'.

'Don't be silly' could be used as a phrase to metaphorically pour cold water on any number of 'transgressions' including crying, becoming a vegetarian, voting Labour, not having a border as part of your wallpapering, not having a border of flowers in your garden, not pulling your curtains to in the morning, using herbs, using mood lighting, worrying about the environment and generally having emotions.

If the *Daily Mail* built a theme park, it would probably look a bit like Bromley. In our house, this paper was faithfully delivered every day (except Sundays). 'Red top' newspapers like the *Sun* and the *Mirror* were seen as very downmarket, but the *Daily Mail* was different, the name itself written in actual Tudor writing. It was as proper and regal as the Magna Carta, or perhaps the menu of a small tea-room like The Silver Lounge in nearby Orpington – a place where my mum, nan and I would get a Black Forest gateau from a clear plastic flap-hatch and a cup of tea served in a small stainless steel teapot, while watching people crossing the precinct with their shopping from Peacocks (which my grandmother would always refer to as 'Pea-coes' – I think because it sounded too rude otherwise).

When I was young, newspapers were still 'outing' celebrities for being gay or for being anything at all, really. I remember as a teenager reading the outrage in the *Mail* about a forthcoming gay drama on Channel 4 called *Queer As Folk* that contained gay men having actual sex.

Aside from gleaning as much as possible from newspapers, from the age of five I had been busy learning about the world by listening into any adult conversations I could. 'Oh, he's so well behaved, isn't he?' my mum's friends would say, looking at me sat quietly at the end of the sofa. I wondered how they could be so naïve. I was quiet because I was busy listening to every word they said – the plans to get the kitchen done if they could afford it; the anger based on something in the news; the sighting of Cheryl Baker in the local supermarket – 'I said, "Hello, Cheryl, all right?" and she said, "Oh hello, all right?" Now, isn't that lovely?' – the 'women's troubles' and Joyce's unloving marriage, leading to my grandmother calling her 'Poor Joyce', to which my mother would say, 'Poor? She's been on a cruise!'

I was very good at being on my best behaviour and tried to never get 'overemotional' or throw a tantrum. Back then, a tantrum was another form of 'showing off', which was frowned upon by my parents because it could 'show them up'. There was a lot of fear around showing off and showing up, though what was being shown was never mentioned. I think Mum and Dad were keen to not be perceived as 'bad parents' – even though nothing could be further from the truth – or as the sort of people who might have badly behaved kids.

I distinctly remember being sat at the bar in a pub one Sunday when I was about seven years old. (I wasn't going to bars aged seven, of course; I was taken there because my dad has always loved going to the pub and back then it was completely fine to plonk your child at the bar with a bottle of Coke and some Mini Cheddars.) My dad's favourite pub was adorned with brass horseshoes, framed pictures of naval battles and tasselled lamps attached to the flock wallpaper on the walls.

Sat at the end of the bar, I, as ever, enjoyed not showing off and felt like I was one of the grown-ups – preferably one of the strong, empowered women I had occasionally glimpsed on soap operas who were always, it seemed, perched at the bar drinking a clear drink with a slice of lemon from a stemmed glass. I loved it because, like my mum's coffee mornings with her friends, I could listen to my dad talk to his mates – men he'd known for years, like Alan the Bag (he sold bags at the market), who had the deepest voice of anyone I'd ever met, which was great for telling stories – once he described a Yorkshire pudding so vividly I could almost taste it.

Dad would often lapse into his London vernacular when down the pub. In winter, he'd say things like, 'It's cold enough for a handbag!' which I assumed was some sort of South London slang for 'very cold', but whenever I've repeated it to any other Londoner – or any other human being, in fact – it's been met with total and utter bemusement.

It being a pub, there were always other people there for me to observe, which was made easier because drunks love talking loudly. On one occasion, I became aware of a man behind me with rosy cheeks, swilling his beer around in his pint glass. 'Well, if it was up to me,' he began, 'I'd put them all on an island. Thing is, within one generation it'd be empty! They'd all be gone! They can't procreate, can they? There'd be no one left! That's why they want to convert one's like him . . .' He gestured to me as I delicately placed a Mini Cheddar on my tongue and took a sip from the straw in my stemmed glass.

The man somehow didn't realise I'd already been 'converted', which, if nothing else, was testament to his lack of perceptiveness and one of the many reasons I assume that things were seldom 'up to him'. Looking back, I wish I could have told him about the islands we have already populated – they're literally to die for! We don't need to procreate, because people flock there – Lindsay Lohan to Mykonos, the Kardashians to Fire Island and several professional football players I've heard about to Gran Canaria.

Another Sunday afternoon, I felt so confident, ensconced at the bar like Angie in *EastEnders*, enjoying crisps and the occasional chit-chat with the barmaid. 'You know Cheryl Baker lives near Bromley – what do you think about that?' She didn't think anything about that, she seldom had much to say, she just kept polishing glasses. It didn't matter though. I sat there imagining my shoulder pads (I was in a green-and-red-striped zip-up tracksuit at the time), with my legs crossed at the knee, Coke through a straw in one hand, crisp in the other.

'Right then, let's get you home, Mum will have dinner ready,' said my dad, patting me on the shoulder. I suddenly had an idea, and I knew exactly what to do to impress everyone – I'd seen it on *EastEnders*. I promptly swung round, looked at my dad with a disdainful stare and then slapped him straight across the face.

Everyone stopped and stared, presumably because they'd never seen such poise and conviction. I didn't see the problem – people were always doing this on TV. Even though I was only seven, I felt certain I could be nominated for a *TV Quick* Award.

The landlord looked over, shocked at my unusual outburst, and crowed, 'You're barred!' and Dad grabbed me by the arm and marched me out of the pub.

'How could you? What were you thinking?!' My dad said as we sat in the car, me in the back, him in the driver's seat (obviously). He turned on the ignition and Whitney Houston blared out of the car stereo because Dad loved playing her in the car. 'I Wanna Dance with Somebody' was the song; Dad didn't want to dance with anybody. He snapped the volume down. I didn't know what to say – I didn't know why I had done it. Maybe I thought it would be funny, or dramatic – I thought this was the sort of behaviour expected from people in pubs.

We didn't go to the pub for a while after that.

In 1992, a new dawn broke over Bromley, which made it no longer dull – it was to have something extraordinary. It was called a 'shopping centre', and in true Bromley fashion some locals lamented the change and preferred the old 'high street' with its slippery trip-hazard pavements. Presumably these were the same people who complained when McDonald's first opened in Market Square because it brought the area down and they were worried about people sliding over on slices of gherkins thrown on the pavement.

The council took over the car park at the back of Marks and Spencer's food hall (a food hall – *never* a supermarket) and built our new shopping centre calling it 'The Glades'. It had an Everglades theme, even though the Everglades have no connection to Bromley, and I don't know if the state of Florida would have been up for twinning with our suburb. While The Glades had a mysterious glamour about it, the main thing was that we could go to Marks & Spencer without going outside. We also now had an Our Price music shop and a food court, which meant you could have Mexican food and Pizza Hut slices all on one tray and we loved it, all of it.

On certain Thursdays after school, Mum would take my brother and I to The Glades in matching outfits (after she'd had her hair done), and we'd peruse things like bath pearls in The Body Shop. Actually, *I* would peruse bath pearls in The Body Shop and my brother would look bored. I would also gaze longingly at the brightly coloured sweaters in The Sweater Shop, the 'jazzy' socks in The Sock Shop and maybe even the 'kooky' ties in The Tie Rack (shops of this era weren't very imaginative with their names).

My favourite shop was Debenhams because it had a spiral staircase with a brass bannister, and I felt like I was Fred Astaire on a helter-skelter as I'd make my way down – even though I was surrounded by boot-cut jeans and electrical items. After a tour of the shops, we would go to McDonald's for tea, and this was fabulous.

Despite all this enchanted glamour, it was nothing in comparison to what they built next to the shopping centre. It was a place they called a 'Leisure Centre' and it was christened 'The Pavilion'. It was a centre for leisure, and it had bright-coloured swirly carpets and sofas in the windows where people could sit and look out of the windows and the management didn't worry about vandalism.

What was remarkable about it all was that everyone was welcome – you didn't have to be a member or even be good at sport; there was an activity for everybody to do from swimming to tanning to sitting down looking out of the window.

The nirvana of the leisure centre was something they called the 'subtropical paradise'. We knew it was subtropical because it had a palm tree made of plastic, a huge window overlooking the dual carriageway and across one wall, an Amazonian display of plants culminating in a waterfall under which people would go to get fingered. The swimming paradise was a place where the shame of being a human being could finally be shaken off in favour of a few hours of unbridled joy. You could hear the cries of delight echoing round the tiled cavern mixed with the chlorinated smell of bacon and bleach. It was a wonderful time to be alive.

There was a café on a balcony overlooking the subtropical paradise, where swimmers and non-swimmers could get a juice, some Wheat Crunchies or even something hot. In effect, this meant you could be walking across wet tiles and then slip on a chip. Scalding yourself with your hot chocolate.

My grandmother, Eileen, who would never go swimming and whom I only ever saw wearing a dress, would be sat in the balcony café, happy with a copy of *Take a Break* magazine, overlooking the swimming pool.

Nan, (as she was to us) was born on the south side of Chicago to Irish parents in 1920, but was brought up on the west coast of Ireland in County Mayo after her father died building the Chicago subway when she was two and her mother returned home. Her mother died shortly after and any money they had was lost in the Wall Street Crash. She was brought up by her Aunty Bea, who nan described as strict, with 'a shock of white hair' that was so white it glowed in the dark – you could see it coming up the road. You wouldn't be allowed to laugh though – not in front of my nan, who was always deeply respectful and grateful to Aunty Bea for bring-ing her up at a time when, as Nan said, 'Everyone knew what it was to go to bed hungry'. This story was frequently retold to my brother and I when we didn't want to eat shepherd's pie, which, sadly, I still don't like.

Moving to England during the war to work in the muni-tions factories, she met my grandfather, moved to London and worked as a home help, caring for people in the community who needed it. Bringing up my mum and aunty in a flat, my grandparents were adamant that their daughters didn't make any noise that might disturb the neighbours, draw attention or bring shame upon my grandfather, who everyone knew from his job in the Post Office.

My grandfather, from Derry, died three years before I was born, and I remember spending a lot of time running around at his grave when I was about three or four, asking questions about this man I'd never met as my mother and grandmother swept and polished the headstone and placed new plants and flowers – still keeping up appearances for him even in death.

Despite living in the UK for much longer than she lived in Ireland, Nan never lost her accent. She was full of eccentricities and was a fiercely proud woman, who worried about her hair being perfect even to go to the hairdressers. Once she went out to the newsagent to buy a copy of the *Sunday Mirror* where a man heard her speak and, because it was during the IRA bombings in London, decided to point at a headline and tell my grandmother, 'This is all your lot's doing! I hope you're bloody happy!'

After this, in her typically proud fashion, she vowed to never speak in public again. Apart from when she would take me to a corner to whisper at me her catchphrase: 'I'm worried about you!' which she would say regardless of the situation. The catchphrase was then immediately repeated to my mum as 'I'm worried about that boy'.

When my aunt once casually mentioned to her about 'homosexuals' she'd been reading about in one of her magazines, my grandmother said she didn't know anything about them – 'Well, we never had them in Ireland!' which I don't think was entirely true.

I think a lot of families have these stories of working people always expected to ride the waves of whatever wars or famines or economic downturns happen to be blowing through. With no cash and no agency to control their circumstances, I imagine all those ancestors from my family tried to get through the day as best they could, and when you have very little, all you cling to is the respect of the people around you. The fear of losing it is, I suppose, what we call 'shame'.

As ever, the blame gets paid forward. It is the generations who follow who still carry the feelings of worry and shame that were bred generations before in economic and social hardship.

The bill gets sent to the wrong address, yet there's still a feeling it must be paid.

Now my grandmother could sit in the balcony café and watch us, her precious kin, not riding ocean waves between America, Ireland and England, desperate for shelter, but fake waves in a subtropical paradise in Bromley.

In this fabulous, glamorous 'swimming pool' designed to look like the sea (if the sea had been tiled), everyone waited for one thing: the wave machine.

The wave machine was heralded by a siren which sounded a bit like this: 'AAAHAAAAAAAAAA', and when you heard that siren, it didn't matter where you were, everyone would come wading into the water – wading with their hands held aloft for balance (and to avoid slipping on a chip), held so high like they were coming to be baptised.

Everyone would be there too – you'd see the whole community represented: your teachers, alongside your dad's friends from the pub and even mum's friend Poor Joyce would be there, looking sad, but still there.

The swimming pool was sloped, like the sea, which meant you could wade into the water up to wherever you felt most comfortable; up to your knees, to your thighs, to your hips, it didn't matter – everyone was welcome. And when the wave machine really got going, the best thing it would make you do was make you jump about three inches off the base of the pool and then back again. The waves of this pretend sea carrying all our fears and anxieties away amongst shrieks of laughter and excitement as the waves lifted us high into the air and delivered us back down again.

Of course, the wave machine would end – as all good things must – and you'd know it had ended because the motion in the ocean would slow and you'd be aware of a wave of plasters floating in on the tide. (Perhaps through baptism the people had been healed.)

Dad loved taking us here – a strong swimmer who had won competitions when he was at school after teaching himself to swim in a pond. He was born in 1941 and growing up during the largest conflict humankind has ever known, I imagine, was quite different to the world I precociously came to know. A world of 'likes' for a photograph of my face, where a 'job' can involve an office with a slide and 'brunch' can be served on a wooden board – as though it's fun to pretend there aren't enough plates.

My dad grew up in Penge, a suburb in South London. People laugh at its name because it sounds rude. Dad also likes to correct me when I say he's from Penge: 'No! How dare you, I'm not from Penge – I'm from Anerley!' not realising that this sounds much worse.

My dad's dad left him and his mum when he was about three years old to run off with another woman. Except there was nowhere to run in 1944, so his mum would see him with his new partner and shout out of the window at them. Dad told me once about how he and his mum would have to walk to the town hall on Saturday mornings to collect the one pound his father was supposed to deposit as child support, but more often than not he'd failed to pay in. They'd walk back with less than no money.

My dad's mum was adopted, but not in the modern sense – there were no interviews or forms to be filled in. She'd been born to a touring actress at the Penge Empire Theatre, but with all the travel she was unable to care for her newborn, so the baby was left with wardrobe mistress and clairvoyant, Lucy, who brought her up as one of her own. Dad and his mum lived in one room at the top of Lucy's house in Penge where, according to dad, they were always very happy and the house was full of love and laughter and Lucy's friends arriving for endless seances. Dad also liked to tell me there was no running water on the top floor until Dad himself plumbed it in.

Occasionally there will be mention of his 'old man' and how he wasn't there for Dad. On one school trip to the local baths (called 'baths' because, alongside swimming, they were a place for people without a bathroom to go upstairs and bathe), there' had been a swimming gala of sorts. The other boys had their dads there to cheer them on, but Dad didn't and not knowing what to do after his swimming race just went home on his own. The next day, the school assembly stopped to give him a round of applause because he'd left without realising he'd won. As you can imagine, the swimming pool was a very important place for Dad – a happy place.

I think this also meant he struggled with my sheer panic at having to get dressed publicly in the changing room where benches lined the walls and everyone could see each other's bits. Even at home, I could never let myself be without clothes.

Desperate to shield myself from imaginary prying eyes, I'd create elaborate changing rituals that meant getting ready for swimming took ages. Swimming trunks laid out on the bench ready for when the towel would be wrapped around me, held at the side in one hand while the other deftly took off my pants and then without letting anyone see through the parting at the side, pick up the trunks, thread my legs through the leg holes and hoist up the trunks as high as possible. Releasing the towel at the last minute to do the last bit of hoisting while the towel became actually stuck in the trunks – it didn't matter, as long as everything was covered.

'No one's looking at you!' my parents would say whenever they encountered this bizarre and elaborate ritual, embarrassed that maybe I was 'making a fuss'. 'Do you think what you've got is special in some way? Oh, that's why we can't see it – I see! He's got a special one!'

Of course, that wasn't what I thought – it was the opposite. I couldn't articulate this though, because no one was as confused as me – I was still looking for that manager to speak to: 'I'm forty-six years old and this has all been a huge mistake!' Trying to make sense of it now, I realise this behaviour was born out of anxieties about the strange thoughts creeping into my mind, about feeling different, which I had no way to understand, and about shame about even having a body at all. It felt like a way to protect myself, but from what, I didn't know.

I think to my dad, a stickler for timekeeping, this was a waste of time and, even worse, a waste of energy. 'Get in the pool and enjoy yourself!' he'd shout, meaning 'Stop worrying and get on with your life!' which isn't bad advice, it's just sometimes difficult to apply when you're trying to keep your balance as you manoeuvre a towel in one hand and swimming trunks in the other. Worse still, none of the other kids seemed that bothered – they were totally carefree, running around with no clothes on, arms up in the air to be towelled down by a parent or seemingly anyone. For me, this was impossible.

At the subtropical paradise, after the wave machine, there was only one thing left – an invention we'd never seen before called 'flumes'. Flumes were big water slides with one special feature: they went *outside* of the building because, as anyone will tell you, nothing is more exciting than being on a water slide over a car park.

My brother and I would be dispatched to go on the flumes on our own. My younger brother would lead the way as he's always been naturally good at sport and is much more confident as a person than I am. When we went on holiday, for example, he'd make friends with the other kids almost as soon as the plane touched down – even with kids who didn't speak the same language. I, on the other hand, did not need friends because I had my parents – and sometimes random adults I'd meet at the hotel breakfast buffet – to talk to.

Dad has always been very keen on challenging us to take leaps of independence, and the flumes were the perfect opportunity. There were two flumes, but one always seemed to be closed because, according to false rumours, 'Last week, somebody *died*'. (It seemed a bit far-fetched that people would die on a water slide, but you didn't question it.) You'd have to wait in a queue on the stairs, which meant standing in your swimming trunks, usually starting to feel a bit chilly. You were basically standing on a staircase, in your underwear, getting cold, which is quite an unusual feeling unless you have a lot of affairs.

The flumes were 'managed' by a bored-looking teenager in a yellow polo shirt who I imagine was also a Venture Scout and carried himself with a very superior air. He also had a whistle, but beyond this I don't know what made him qualified for the job. You'd have to wait for what felt like eternity until it was your turn – your special moment – on the flumes. When you were at the top of the line, you'd be called forward. A small feeling of trepidation might creep in, but you knew you'd come so far that you couldn't turn back, and besides, the sixteen-year-old would have a look of annoyed impatience about him (which, incidentally, he did not have when girls his own age were feeling trepidatious), meaning you had no choice.

Like any protective older brother with a deeply ingrained sense of fear about everything, I'd bravely suggest to my brother that he should go first. He'd be flying down the flumes in no time, screaming delightedly, and I'd hear Dad cheering in the landing pool far below.

Then it would be time for my go. When it was your turn on the flumes, you'd have to sit in place at the top and wait, while cascades of water flew out from under you, which were designed to lubricate your passage, as it were. The sixteen-year-old would be glaring at you while waiting for a small traffic light to turn from red to green (why we weren't trusted with just watching the traffic light ourselves is anyone's guess). Eventually, to herald your special moment, the sixteen-year-old would turn to you and say, in an insouciant tone, 'You can go now if you want . . .'

On this day, I launched myself off with a surge of pride that I'd once again overcome my fears. The flumes were made of tubes of plastic that had been bolted together, and as you went over these joins, they felt like they were cutting into your back like knives (some people said gangs put razor blades in them but even I knew this wasn't true). Because I'd been waiting for so long, I ignored these minor irritations – grinning with delight but also saying, 'Huh!' and then, 'Ouch,' at each one, but not too loudly.

Being a flimsy nine-year-old with no real momentum, I would find myself slowing to a standstill mid-flume. I had built up no velocity, and the jets of water just weren't enough somehow. Panic set in. Despite trying to scooch myself forward it was to no avail – I was stuck. I tried to keep myself calm. *The sixteen-year-old upstairs was the last person to see me – he wouldn't leave me here, he'll come for me. He'll send for me . . . surely?*

Still, I was unable to move. Was this it? Was I dead? Was there a light I was moving towards? Oh no, that was just the car park.

And then at that moment, any serenity was shattered as I saw over my head, the shadow of somebody else moving through the flume tube behind me. Desperately, I scrambled again to get moving again. Still nothing. I looked over my shoulder, gradually surrendering to the situation as the toes of someone else came round the corner, followed by the legs of someone else and then, finally, the face of someone else. And that was when I realised it was, of course, my mum's friend Joyce. Poor Joyce! Her one attempt at having a simple moment of joy – carefree for one short second amongst the screeches and shrieks of pleasure all around her – ruined by my presence.

She smashed into the back of me at great speed, and suddenly we were both hurtling along together, me nestled in the bosom of her thighs, both of us moving now at double-speed, our combined weights taking our momentum to a now strato-spheric level. Both of us screaming – I think now, for different reasons. Round one corner, then the next, both of us being flung from one side to the other – when would it ever end?! *Would* it ever end? Then, finally, we were thrown out of the end of the flumes across the sky, past the fake palm trees, past my grandmother on the balcony, past the window overlooking the dual carriageway and crashed with a profound splash in the landing pool.

As we both came back up for air after being plunged into the water, we looked at each other in a way that said, 'I never expected to touch like that!' and which also said, 'We will *never* speak of this again.'

And that was when I first realised that I was gay.

2

Speaking

I've always had to explain myself.

'Why do you talk like that?' asked the girl with gold hooped earrings and a fringe that had been curled with tongs but also gelled to stick to the top of her face. She had a black bomber jacket on with the name of a record label embroidered across the back. It's so strange to me now that the London garage scene could be combined with embroidery. It was from the market in Orpington – everyone got their coats there. Her name was Felicity but she didn't say it like that, it was more 'Feliss-iteeee'.

It was autumn 1996, I was thirteen years old and in Year 9. It was the time of Oasis, Blur and, in South London, the phenomenon of garage music. I never understood what 'garage music' was other than a response to 'house music', but I didn't understand what 'house music' was (and why no one ever went into the garden). Perhaps it's obvious that I didn't know much about it, even now, because I add 'music' to the end, like a parent who still says 'disco' instead of 'club'.

I knew that garage music had something to do with the raves advertised on luminous cardboard signs strung to lamp-posts near roundabouts and also something to do with pirate radio, which seemed to have little to do with men with parrots on their shoulders and much more to do with people shouting from their bedrooms on distorted frequencies between the main radio stations on the FM dial. I knew I wouldn't like this music and I wouldn't enjoy going to any of those roundabout raves because when I say the 'main radio stations', I mean BBC Radio 2 and BBC Radio 4. I sought out these stations for late-night book readings to help me sleep and Sunday-afternoon shows that had songs from the musicals. At the age of thirteen, not only did I feel like I was forty-six, I also had the listening tastes of a seventy-five-year-old gay man who runs an antiques shop in Hampshire.

Not that I'd ever openly admit then to preferring musical theatre over garage music. That would be deemed 'sad'. Sad was the worst thing you could be. It didn't mean emotionally sad (though actually all the people trying to fit in did look emotionally sad), being sad meant that you were unaware of what was happening in the world, you'd been left behind by the times, you were an outsider with no friends – you were a 'sad case'. It could range from the big to the small: not gelling your fringe to your face, choosing to button up your blazer or wearing your backpack on both shoulders were all examples of being 'sad'. A girl in my form group, Tiffany, wore her bag on both shoulders, which led to her being labelled 'Tizzy Two Straps' for ever more. Poor Tizzy. In fact, I think I came up with that to deflect from my love of musicals. What a sad case poor Tizzy was. Though now she's probably not sad at all because, unlike her peer group, she doesn't have to deal with sciatica.

My school had been built in the 1960s, like most secondary school comprehensives in the UK. It had lots of concrete, wood and glass and, every now and then, some big, billowy curtains with bold, psychedelic prints on them. It was a brutalist building, which no doubt added to the sense of brutality in the school. Concrete and glass don't encourage feelings – they encourage you to not stick out. I mean this quite literally because if you did stick out, you'd bash into something hard. Like concrete, wood or glass. Flamboyance was not just dangerous socially, but also physically.

The maths corridor was especially depressing because it had the most holes in the walls. They weren't the result of a war, but of kids who'd been thrown out of their maths lesson for doing something disgusting, like spitting balled-up paper out of their mouth, or something cheeky, like asking the sixty-three-year-old maths teacher out on a date, or something disruptive, like upending a chair. Being thrown out was hardly a punishment if you hated being there in the first place. The naughty boys always managed to smuggle a compass out with them somehow and then used the spiky end to chisel into the wall, bizarrely, as though they were trying to tunnel back into the classroom they'd so hated being in just a moment before.

Our school was thought to be very lucky because, despite the holes in the wall in the maths corridor, in the PE department we had a tiny swimming pool, which the Parent-Teacher Association had saved up for from endless raffles and cheese 'n' wine evenings. Combining cheese with wine was, at this point, seen as the height of sophistication and not something people could do in their own homes – it had to be sanctioned by the PTA.

Due to the indoor pool being built in the middle of the staff car park, it had to be very long and yet very narrow – barely as wide as a single-lane road. Despite this, to incorporate the twenty-five boys in each swimming class, we had to line up along the length of the pool to do widths. In keeping with its small size, there were only two sets of steps at either end, so we were expected to be able to hoist ourselves out of the side of the swimming pool without the steps, which everyone knows is nearly impossible, especially as I had such delicate hands from playing the piano.

Needless to say I was very bad at this, and my effort largely involved getting one knee up on the side and then dragging myself up from this position, clawing at the shiny tiled floor as I did so. I was always last. How did the other boys know how to do it? I wondered if it was something they got taught at football practice.

At the time, I was under a lot of pressure from my piano teacher to get better at my scales (where you drag your fingers up and down the piano in various permutations of the black and white keys), but there never seemed to be enough time to practise. Also, it felt like there was pressure from all directions – remembering swimming kit, taking in food to cook in food tech, carrying ring binders bigger than my torso, having enough money for the bus and for lunch, in addition to learning how to get out of a swimming pool.

The other major distraction here was fancying boys, and nowhere was this more of an issue than in swimming. To stop myself getting 'distracted' by the other boys in my class, I came up with an ingenious plan – like so many gays before me, I would combine sexual repression with piano practice. I decided that as soon as my mind drifted to one of my classmates, I'd begin reciting my scales, usually in my head but sometimes by mistake out loud. It was quite something to be lusting after someone and then immediately replace that fantasy with a G-minor contrary-motion scale. It must have made the other boys think I was doubly strange that whenever they walked past in their trunks I would burst into '*G! A! B flat! C, D, E flat! F sharp!*'

On particularly lustful weeks, my piano teacher would be astonished that I would be suddenly flawless at these scales. Like so many things at the time, I couldn't explain it.

So there I was, at break-time, having to answer questions about my voice again. 'I don't know why I speak in this voice – I've always spoken like it. I didn't plan it. I just spoke.' For some reason, since I learnt to talk, I've had a posh voice. I still don't know why.

'Are your family posh?'

'No.'

'Are you gay?'

'No!'

'Felicity leave him alone – that's just the way he talks, OK?'

'I ain't saying it's a bad fing!'

Feliss-iteeee was the new friend of my friend, Cindy. Cindy had decided she was my best friend because we had the same piano teacher. She had a straight fringe (not gelled), braces on her teeth and she worked hard at school. Her mum had exactly the same hair but wore lovely bright-red lipstick – you could see it even when the sun shone on her car windscreen.

The music department had teachers who were a bit like the French Resistance during the Second World War. They were eccentric and funny and often provided a safe haven for outsiders in the school. The staff included a piano teacher, Mr Rollings, who managed to make his hair stand on end away from his face without hair gel, which was in stark contrast to everyone else at the school.

He conducted a church choir at the weekends and refused

to call anyone by an abbreviation of their name, so I had to be 'Thomas'. He carried his sheet music in a doctor's bag, which gave him the air of a life-saving musician. Though, in contrast with his formal shoes and formal names, he also wore a Tommy Hilfiger duvet jacket, so he was full of surprises.

The music rooms were a refuge for me and my other closeted homosexual friends – though none of us had the courage to acknowledge that we were gay. I can't stress enough how unthinkable this would have been. Apart from the social hang-ups about what coming out would mean, Section 28 was in full force at this time. If you're not familiar, the Thatcher government had created a clause in the Local Government Act of 1988, which meant publicly funded schools could not 'promote homosexuality' or 'promote the teaching in any maintained school of the acceptability of homosexuality as a pretended family relationship'. Basically, a teacher could lose their job if they told you it was OK to be gay or even brought up the subject.

The music rooms were next to the playground, where the other boys played football and the muddy ball would often ricochet off the cage that covered our windows on one side, but it was a place where we could be ourselves – even though 'ourselves' at this stage was largely re-enacting Victoria Wood sketches, prancing around and speaking fast and, often, cleaning. I remember one lunchtime, I thought I was being very funny singing 'Do You Hear The People Sing' from *Les Misérables* while picking up waste paper off the floor in what would now be described as the 'Bend and Snap'. I then turned round to see no one was laughing – which, precociously, I found disconcerting – and then realised a boy from the year above was standing in the doorway.

'Why do you bend over like that?' he asked, bemused but in an angry way.

'I was just bending over to pick up the paper off the floor,' I said, quietly.

'Why don't you bend over and pick it up normally then?'

'I, I do.'

He glared at me. 'Gay!' he shouted and slammed the door. He'd been accurate, if intimidating, and we didn't laugh for the rest of that lunchtime.

Piano lessons were conducted in small rooms off the music corridor, which were like prison cells if prison cells were furnished with pianos (and maybe they are, I have never been). Most people learning the piano are preparing for their grade exams, which involve playing some set pieces of music, some scales and then doing aural exercises. This was the cause of much sniggering because it sounds like 'oral'. But there was no sniggering in my piano lessons. It was devastating when I'd have to stand in the corner of the cell while Mr Rollings played a tune that I'd then have to sing back. I hated my speaking voice so much that using it to sing was agonising.

My self-proclaimed best friend, Cindy, never came to be part of the lunchtime gay socials, especially since Felicity was now on the scene. I'd noticed Cindy had started dropping her 'T's and seemed to be moving towards block heels, rather than sensible flat loafers. They'd also taken to going to The Glades shopping centre in Bromley to 'get off' with boys at the week-end. I knew that loosely meant kissing, but beyond that I wasn't sure because I was rarely invited any more.

They may not sound like great friends, but my experience of secondary school was akin to being sent to prison. Aside from the Liberace-esque piano cells, school was a long stretch; there was no getting out of it, and somehow I had to survive. The fact that Cindy had announced herself as my best friend made it a little easier – I was just grateful to have someone to talk to at break-times because being on your own would mean people would think you were a 'loner' and therefore extremely 'sad'. Even Tizzy Two Straps had her group of friends to talk to. Though I worked hard to suppress all my feelings, Cindy preferring to spend time with Felicity did feel like a blow.

However, Felicity's arrival would have to be put up with, even if it meant I had to answer more questions on why I spoke differently. It was a question I've had to answer for as long as I've been able to speak. Truth be told, I don't know why I have this posh voice. My mum and dad grew up in South London and spoke just like every other Londoner. When my brother came along, he spoke the same as them. The other kids at school thought I was looking down my nose at them and yet I wasn't (yet), and I certainly didn't know anyone who was actually posh to hang out with, so I was stuck in the middle of nowhere.

My mum loved it though and would take any opportunity to thrust me in front of people to just say something – 'I don't know where we got him from, really!'

My school did not take kindly to this sort of flamboyance; it was different to being a 'sad case' – if anything it was too far the other way. For example, a boy four years older than me called Johnny had got a job in a hairdresser's on a Saturday. Like me, he had a different voice, though his was higher pitched and each sentence went down at the end. He couldn't walk down a corridor without people rasping out, 'Johneeeeeeee,' with a bent wrist, followed by the expression, 'Hello, boys!'

'Hello, boys' was something people at my school assumed all gay people said, all the time, which was ridiculous because if gay men were surrounded by other gay men they wouldn't need to keep referencing that they were all boys. Instead of 'Hello, boys', they'd just say 'Hello', but school bullying has never been governed by reason. I can only imagine how horrible it must have been. If asked about his sexuality, Johnny would bravely say, 'I don't know what I am really,' but other people knew, and they weren't happy about it. I remember him walking down a corridor, hunched over with his face in his hands just to avoid all the jeering. I don't know if he felt vulnerable, I always thought he seemed so grown-up. I mean, after all, he had a Saturday job in a hairdresser's, which seemed so glamorous. However, I also knew I had to see him as a warning: *This is how people will treat me if I become too noticeable.*

There was a school canteen, which was suitably grim. The art department had made an effort to adorn the walls with work by promising students, but even that spark of joy had been undermined by having food thrown at it. There was one painting of a girl in Year 11, gazing pensively at her rulers and maths equipment in front of her. Her serene demeanour was despite the fact that someone had chosen to throw a slice of cucumber at her face. This bright slice of green was, I suppose, deemed too flamboyant for the beige of the tuna-mayonnaise sandwich from which it had been thrown. That cucumber was there from when I was in Year 7 until I left in Year 13.

It was in the canteen that I came to understand I wasn't blending in as much as I thought. I'd been fancying other boys – I think it's fair to say at some point I'd fancied *all* the other boys. This had been going on since approximately midway through Year 7, when I was eleven and three quarters.

In the canteen – this veritable brasserie of our suburban prison – barriers had been concreted to the floor to organise the queuing system. One break time in Year 8 I was standing there in the slow-moving crush of the queue and I noticed a boy come into the seating area of the canteen next to the barriers. I was standing in the line, reciting scales in the key of A-flat major over three octaves. I noticed this boy because he was angry and had hair in a bowl cut. He bounced in with two of his friends, and because I like noticing things, I glanced at him.

'Why you fucking looking at me?!' he hollered. I stared back blankly, so he repeated, '*Why* you fucking looking at me?!'

I wasn't! Why were there always so many questions? I mouthed back incredulously, 'What?'

'Stop looking at me!' It made me feel like cold water was running up and down my spine. I looked away and carried on waiting for the queue to move. The truth is, I didn't even need to buy anything. I just needed to do something and be somewhere at break-time because I had nowhere else to go and didn't want to look like a sad-case loner. I had felt increasingly out of place with Cindy and Feliss-iteeee as they had so much to discuss regarding their new hobby of 'getting off with boys' and the fear that if they got off with too many, they'd be labelled 'slags' but if they didn't get off with boys at all, they might be labelled 'frigid'.

Frigid, slag, gay, sad-case, two-straps – there was really no winning for anyone.

I bought a doughnut. The ones they sold in the canteen were massive and covered in thick white icing. They tasted mainly of fat, but everyone ate them so I did too, just to fit in.

Sometimes I'd just have one of these for lunch because I was too ashamed to eat anything like a sandwich in case it had some flamboyant cucumber in it – an instant giveaway of my homosexual tendencies –and I feared I'd immediately get over-excited and start singing a G-minor arpeggio, badly.

My dad took to making me a ham sandwich most days, but I often felt too embarrassed to eat it and would wait until I got home, as though people might say, 'Oh my God! You're so sad – your dad makes you a sandwich!' Even the idea of being loved by my dad felt like a flamboyance I needed to hide. Love in any form felt like it was something to be ashamed of.

I left the canteen to get my bag from the bag rack – basically, a series of shelves under a covered walkway housing everyone's two-strapped-backpacks and embroidered record bags. There was no one there except me as I bent over to retrieve my backpack.

'*I told you to stop fucking looking at me!*'

'What?' I said, turning. 'But I didn—'

Before I managed to complete the sentence, the small angry boy from the canteen managed to jump-kick me against the wall. I didn't know how he managed to fly across the air like that into my chest – he could have been a dancer, if only he'd channelled his energies. I felt the impact across my ribs but told myself I could take it – they were just shoes and legs flying at me after all.

He flew at me again.

'Why did you look at me?'

Another kick. And another.

I was cowered against the wall by this point. Not on the floor, but my back up against the bricks, my shoulders hunched protectively, my arms half folded across my chest, pathetically.

No longer a forty-six-year-old trapped in a child's body. I was just a child.

'Stop fucking looking at me, you little gay!'

He walked off with his mates. I was furious, but only at myself. I thought I'd done a good job of covering everything up – only ever using one strap on my backpack, unbuttoning my blazer, not eating cucumbers, making sure I didn't look at the other boys for too long and not getting excited about boys I saw in the maths corridor. Perhaps it was this stupid voice that had given me away. Maybe I was looking at the other boys more than I realised. I thought I'd done my best, serving my time, acting pretty grown-up. Now though there was nowhere to hide; I'd run out of scales, all the instruments playing all the scales in the world couldn't help me now.

Play-acting high status and reciting Victoria Wood characters in the music rooms only seemed more ridiculous when suddenly compared to the sheer humiliation of that moment, when you think you've been an adult about everything, but there's no denying you're just a thirteen-year-old boy, cowering against a wall.

Cindy and Feliss-iteeee appeared with their new record bags (did they want people to think they were DJs now?). 'Tom, what happened? Are you OK?'

'I'm fine,' I said hurriedly to stop myself from crying. I walked off along the covered walkway, alone. The bell would ring soon and it would be time for another class.

As I walked into the main school building, Mrs Millar, my formidable head of year and a power house of handling kids thrown out of maths approached me. 'Tom. I heard someone say you'd been crying at break-time and someone had kicked you?'

All I could muster was a repeat of the confused expression that had gotten me into trouble just minutes before. 'Wha—?'

Annoyingly, I've found that I can cower against a wall being kicked and not cry, but someone being nice to me makes me want to sob uncontrollably. I held it together for Mrs Millar though.

'. . . And if you'd like to tell me who it is, I would like to listen because, as you know, we have a policy that bullying is not tolerated at this school.'

Even though this was my lifeline, I knew I absolutely couldn't tell her because I didn't want to make a fuss or make it worse. Somehow I thought I wasn't worth it — things like this were inevitable if I didn't hide myself well enough. I fought back tears and nodded my head and walked off. It was never spoken of again.

If I was unwilling to tell my head of year, the traditional response to getting beaten up might be to get tough, to fight back, to go in the following day and beat the boy right back in retaliation. My dad once tried to get me into boxing by getting me to punch his hands, but I knew I couldn't do it — physical violence sounds ridiculous with my accent. My dad was disappointed as he had high hopes I'd have a natural inclination, but this was mainly down to me wearing a silk dressing gown. With these two options out of the window, I only had one response left: I would take to the stage.

It would be unfair of me to suggest that everything about this time was dull and depressing. The school had lots of wonderful teachers, many of whom were newly qualified and full of energy and loved their job. Every October we would have a school cabaret, which was very exciting for everyone – especially the PTA, who used the interval to sell more cheese and wine, presumably to buy more steps for the swimming pool. The cabaret happened every year on the third Friday in October, like a surprise gift that cropped up just as we were getting back into the swing of the new school year – like a slice of cucumber in a tuna sandwich.

In previous years, a shy German teacher had read a vaguely amusing poem by Pam Ayres and that confident girl, Becky, from Year 10 sung a Barbra Streisand song because she loved Barbra Streisand so much. It was 'so beautiful' people said, clapping. It was only clapping too, as this was before *The X Factor* taught British people to whoop and cheer all the time. I think there was a worry that too much emotion might set the fire alarms off.

I clapped too, while seething bitterly because I desperately wanted to openly love Barbra Streisand, but I knew it would be too flamboyant. Becky had a T-shirt with her face on it, and that was fine. Her dad was such a massive fan that they had all her tapes in the car. We had her tape in the car too, but when I talked about Barbra I'd get overexcited and we'd have to listen to the Carpenters to bring my mood back down.

In the school cabaret, there was always a dance routine performed by a group of sixth-form girls who wore shiny trousers and had crimped hair pulled up by scrunchies. It was usually performed to quite an upbeat yet aggressive song like 'Return of the Mack' by Mark Morrison. The dance routine always had the same two moves – elbows jolted out to the side at chin height and then hands covering up the face while bent forward – in endless combinations.

I knew the school cabaret could be a chance to really do something, to prove myself to those bullies. Admittedly, it was just a school show, but it was all I had. I'm not a particularly vindictive person, and I didn't really want to get revenge on anyone who'd beaten me up. To be honest, I didn't know what I wanted, really, I just knew I wanted to do *something*. Getting on a stage to perform anything is an odd response to being kicked against a wall for merely glancing at another person, but if human beings made sense, I'd be out of a job.

I had to decide on something to perform that wasn't singing, dancing or a Pam Ayres poem. Something like a story, perhaps? That's what I knew I wanted to do. 'You want to do a monologue? But you can't find a monologue? Well, what do you *want* to do?' roared Ms Butcher who was directing the cabaret. She was a brilliant drama teacher and very excitingly wore stage make-up, even in the day, and had bright-red hair that seemed to be sort of spiky and long at the same time so that when she was particularly animated she looked to me like a ghost but also like a firework. I found her quite terrifying but I later realised she just had a louder voice than anyone else I had encountered in Bromley, presumably because she was so good at projection. If I was terrified it was really that I was in awe of her and her high standards and always wanted to impress her, 'Look through this.' She gave me a book of monologues. The thing with monologues is, they're really boring; characters doing something dramatic about living in Russia in a longer story you don't get to see – they're as boring as someone telling you their dreams.

On the shelf behind her desk, I also saw a book with Elton John on the front. I loved Elton John – he was shameless. 'That's not Elton John! That's *Talking Heads* by Alan Bennett!' So, I got to take a copy of his *Talking Heads* monologues too. As I read through a few, I instantly loved them – they weren't boring at all. I realised how much I loved the language, the way he'd captured the way normal people spoke, in the same way that Victoria Wood did. They all sounded like my mum's friends, the people I'd grown up listening to. I didn't know people on stage were allowed to talk like normal people.

The monologue I loved the best was the one performed by Julie Walters called 'Her Big Chance'. I loved Julie Walters from watching her on Victoria Wood's *As Seen On TV* with my mum and from recreating the sketches in the music room with the other gays.

It's a monologue about a young woman who takes herself very seriously as an actor, and she's full of observations about everything except how badly she's being mistreated. She doesn't realise that her big chance in the movies isn't an ordinary film, it's a porn film. I didn't see the poignancy of all this, I just loved the way the character seemed obsessed with the director's tone of voice. I didn't know what a porn film was really, though the *Daily Mail* on the kitchen table at home seemed to be obsessed with 'snuff movies' around this time. I liked the sadness of it the most – a character with thwarted ambitions who struggled with their situation who kept going as best they could. I didn't know authors wrote about people like this.

It didn't cross my mind that this character was a woman and I wasn't. It also didn't really cross my mind that it might not be entirely suitable for a light-hearted school cabaret.

I performed it in a rehearsal in front of the drama-teacher–director and the dance squad in the school hall that had the big billowy patterned curtains. The sun was shining through the window behind them so I couldn't see their faces as I sat on a chair on the stage and read out the monologue. I loved doing it out loud for the first time but no one laughed because apart from anything else it's not really funny, it's mainly tragic.

There was a confused silence at the end. 'Well, you haven't learnt it!' bellowed the teacher. This was true, I hadn't. In retrospect, it is probably more surprising that she didn't pick up on it being a monologue about a porn film. 'Have you even thought about how this character dresses . . . or anything?' I hadn't a clue. I just really liked the way the character talked.

The following morning Dad was driving me to school. 'I don't understand why you have to play a woman – couldn't you do a Roald Dahl poem or something?' Yet again, I was being confronted with questions. I'd foolishly mentioned I'd struggled with doing a funny monologue that wasn't funny. And actually quite tragic. And told by a woman inadvertently appearing in a porn film.

The thing about being in the car for any parental chats is that you can't escape – I was a thirteen-year-old and not Bruce Willis, and therefore had no idea how to 'drop and roll' out of a moving vehicle, which would have looked ridiculous on Summer Hill in Bromley anyway. Once when I was in the car with my dad, he'd asked me, 'You know what a condom is, don't you?' out of *nowhere*, and I wanted to wind down the window and hurl myself out. I just said yes and turned up the Carpenters.

This conversation was no less upsetting. His comment burnt into me – a Roald Dahl monologue? I am not six. This is a sophisticated monologue with wonderful wordplay written by the world's greatest Elton John impersonator, Alan Bennett. There was no use trying to explain myself. We just sat in silence. Apparently, the one place men talk is in the car because they can't get away from each other, but I have always refused to be drawn into doing what other men do.

All these questions were making me more and more determined. After the next rehearsal, I went to the costume store, which was a cupboard that smelled of dead mice. The only dress I could find was a big purple ball gown like Belle wore in *Beauty and the Beast*. It was flouncy and totally inappropriate. I put it on to show I was trying to conform to Ms Butcher's instructions and wore it across the school site to the school hall.

The thing about after-school clubs is that they take place at the exact same time as detention for the naughty kids – the ones who've spent the day throwing cucumber slices and making a mess of the maths corridor's plasterwork. The boy from the year above who'd accosted me for the way I bent over in the music room walked past me. He literally did a double take and then stopped.

It was like he'd been collecting all the aggression and anger in his life for just this moment. 'You fucking poof! You're a fucking poof, you fucking poof.' Unlike Alan Bennett's words, I didn't care for this boy's use of language at all, mainly because it was so repetitive.

I genuinely think he might have just walked past and not shouted if he hadn't been so adamantly programmed to hate everything that I represented at that moment. In a way, I felt bad for him – I'd managed to cram everything he disliked into one thirteen-year-old-sized parcel: a camp kid, from the year below, who not only seemed gay but even had the audacity to wear a dress – a big flouncy, purple, Belle-from-*Beauty-and-the-Beast* ball gown.

Obviously, the dress was wrong and the rehearsal seemed even less funny than the last one – if anything my plan to use this monologue to prove myself was going seriously awry, but I kept thinking I simply had to do it. It was a strange plan, perhaps the strangest plan to overcome bullying ever, but it was my plan. Besides, the school cabaret was on Friday. This was Wednesday; people had bought tickets, they were expecting a show, the PTA was relying on the funds. While I was worried about the response I might get, I knew if I backed out now I may as well go back to being kicked against that wall.

There was another music teacher, Miss Werry, who'd been accompanying Becky on 'Papa, Can You Hear Me?' and sat quietly in the corner for the rehearsal. She found me in my big purple dress going back to the cupboard to get changed.

'Tom, this is all wrong.'

'I know,' I said deflated, like a Disney character on some sort of steps.

'This dress isn't right, but I might have something I can lend you, if you like?'

Miss Werry was a confident person who was petite but tough, because she had a really difficult form group. (I knew this because sometimes they tried to talk on the way into assembly, and she was having none of that.) I think she had lots of gay friends too because she sang in lots of choirs.

'I'll bring it on Friday.'

And she did. After a sleepless forty-eight hours of learning the lines, I sat in awe as she produced a blond wig out of a black box with a very flamboyant red stripe on it and a green sequined mini-dress. I stole a pair of my mum's red leather boots from the wardrobe in our spare room. The music teacher even did my make-up. 'I'm putting a red dot on the edge of each eye, which is what a drag-queen friend of mine taught me to do – it makes your eyes look bigger.'

She even knew drag queens! I couldn't imagine the world she operated in, going outside Bromley, singing in choirs full of gays and drag queens. How many exams would I have to pass to be allowed there?

Young people are often rebuked for not appreciating things like the help they're offered, and I was no different. I think I was so overwhelmed with learning my lines, finding the right outfit, not being too flamboyant but at the same time still being a thirteen-year-old boy dressing up as a woman accidentally appearing in a porn film, that I didn't have a moment to take in just how intuitive this teacher was. During this whole process, she had calmed me down, made time for me and didn't make me feel totally indulgent for attempting to do such an odd choice of monologue (it did feel like a very indulgent thing to do especially as this was before people had learnt emotions from watching *Britain's Got Talent*).

The audience was made up of parents who were very excited to see their own children do something adorable, some other students from the school who'd come to show support for people they fancied and, of course, stood at the back, was the ever industrious PTA. Cindy and Felicity were there mainly because Cindy insisted on it. Felicity thought it was all a bit sad, but it was better than hanging around the bowling alley, trying to get off with boys from the private school up the road.

They had all paid for tickets, the adults bought PTA wine and sat down in the school hall for their Friday-night entertainment. They were just recovering from a very lively Year 11 dance routine to 'Boombastic' by Shaggy, which had followed on from a girl in Year 8 performing 'Memory' from *Cats* on the clarinet. They were getting everything they expected and they loved it. My mum was there with Aunty Jilly (not my real aunt, but a close friend of the family. More on her later), who had always been a big supporter of me doing outlandish performances.

I stepped out onto the stage, awkwardly carrying a chair to sit on. I'd taken it from the maths classroom where I'd been secretly getting ready. I was trying to keep the wig out of my eyes (I have never had much experience with hair) and I was barely able to walk in heels. It was only then that I realised I was terrified. All the rushing around of the last few days, trying to get the lines learnt, had distracted me from this moment.

I should have practised in the heeled boots! I thought to myself but I knew I'd been too embarrassed to practise walking in them because I was worried I'd see that boy from the year above, and I think I was also trying to deny that I was even doing this peculiar monologue at all. As I walked out, I kept thinking that a Roald Dahl poem would have been so much easier.

The spotlight, operated by a tall sixth-former with quite bad acne, blinded me as I walked across the shiny wooden floor of the stage in the main hall, each clipped step ringing out across the room. There was a smattering of laughter – I imagine from embarrassment or perhaps from hilarity at seeing a thirteen-year-old boy in a green sequined mini-dress, but this wasn't the laugh I wanted.

I sat down. The audience stared at me as I started to deliver the story of a deluded porn actress being exploited on a boat in the Solent river with all the intonation I'd learnt from watching Julie Walters. The audience of mums and dads from Bromley seemed bemused.

Maybe they were listening. I kept thinking, *Why am I putting myself through this?* All I knew was that I had to get to the end.

After a massive pause, when they finally realised it was over, they clapped politely and supportively. Maybe somewhat confused. This wasn't a cute performance to be captured on a camcorder. This wasn't an adorable Andrew Lloyd Webber melody played on woodwind. What was this audience supposed to do? They probably wanted to say, 'What the hell was that?!' They wanted a languages teacher doing a vaguely amusing poem.

Even now I think about how perverse it was to feel afraid, and rather than take steps to protect myself, I did the opposite – I did something that could surely only exacerbate the problem.

Afterwards, I got changed and returned the dress to Miss Werry, who helped me take off my make-up too. She smiled. 'You did very well,' she whispered.

'Thanks.'

I went out to the canteen where the PTA were serving cheese and wine to see Mum and Aunty Jilly. Cindy saw me too. 'Yeah, it was good! Didn't expect you to do something in a dress, though.'

'I thought it was well good!' said Felicity, smiling, both of them now apparently reviewers as well as DJs.

'Well, thanks for coming!'

Mum and Aunty Jilly were proud of me – they said they loved it. 'And I liked those shoes – I think I recognise them from somewhere,' said Mum, smiling.

Ms Butcher wrote in my report at the end of the year, *I didn't know if it would work, but it did. Well done, Tom!*

I didn't know why I did it, I just knew I really wanted to, and despite all my better instincts, I did. There's a part of me that has found that if people are going to pick on you for being different, you can either work to blend in so you don't get picked on any more. Or you can go the other way and be as different as you can be, just to show them you won't be cowed against a wall forever. It's not the same as retaliating with physical violence, but it is a giant 'up yours' to anyone who's coming for you. Even if it does feel like freezing cold water running down your spine. You don't do it for anyone else; you do it for yourself.

3

Eating

My mum worked for The Army & Navy. She wasn't in the military – The Army & Navy was a department store on Bromley high street. It was part of House of Fraser, and in our eyes, it was one above shops like Allders and Debenhams. Mum worked in ladies' fashions on the first floor, opposite the lift and next to the wedding hats.

Mum had to stand there for hours at a time, often with very few customers, in the heat of the British summer, which was never alleviated by any air conditioning. The only let-up was that Mum got to work alongside Aunty Jilly, who, whilst not my real aunt, is perhaps the most exuberant person I've ever met. She had red hair in a soft blow wave at the time and wore extravagant leggings and lots of jewellery and would tease Mum that she had a son who didn't speak like her at all. 'Irene! This isn't your son – he speaks like that, and you can't even say "garage" properly – you say "ga-ridge,"' and Mum would fall about laughing.

Mum wasn't allowed to have a handbag at work and had to carry her belongings in a clear plastic bag so the security guards on the staff entrance could spot if she'd stolen anything from the shop floor. (This was the case for all the employees – they hadn't singled her out.)

It was this bag, containing an apple and a compact umbrella, that smashed me in the face as Mum leant over to kiss me goodbye. I was still in bed. Moments before, my bedroom door had burst open in her flurry of rushing to get out of the house and catch the bus that dropped her outside Woolworths so she could hop over the road to the store. This would all have to happen with no margin of error because, like me, my mum has always been late. I think Mum was cutting it so fine because being early just felt like she was giving extra minutes to the job she hated. 'Get out there and enjoy yourself in the sunshine – I wish I could!' exclaimed Mum as she basically ran back out of my room so as not to miss the bus.

It was 1998 and the nation was still reeling from the imprisonment of Deidre Rachid (née Barlow) in *Coronation Street*. Despite seismic events going on in the wider world, Bromley was typically quiet. I had longed for the summer holidays at the end of Year 10, which represented the chance to finally relax after the mock exams in which I had performed terribly. Looking back, this was because my brain was so confused and tired from pushing away what I now deemed my 'undesirable thoughts' about other boys while being expected to retain information about Jane Austen and asexual reproduction in plants. In a way, I wished I was a plant.

I had just turned fifteen. I'm not sure I quite liked it. I had no money because, unlike a lot of my schoolmates who had jobs in their families' businesses, I didn't have a family like that. I'd sometimes walk a neighbour's dog for three quid a time, but I knew that wasn't going to give me my dream lifestyle.

My dream lifestyle at this point involved me living in a stately home (the sort that my mum would take me to for a scone but not to look around the house itself as it was too

expensive), having a MiniDisk Walkman and a television in my
room that I could watch from bed. It also involved lots of travel
and wearing suits – even around the house. So the last two I
can tick off the list now.

At this time, all I wanted to do was sleep. Staying in bed
meant I didn't have to think about the boys at school I fancied
to the point of *pain,* but now couldn't even see across a crowded
maths corridor until September.

Without a job to focus on, the summer holidays felt lonely
because arranging to meet up with people was, for me, fraught
because they might want to spend an afternoon doing something I didn't want to do and then it would just feel like being
back at school. What if they wanted to go to Laser Quest or
wanted me to talk about girls I fancied (who didn't exist) or
join a gang or any number of unpalatable possibilities? Whatever
it was, I'd end up going along with it just to be polite and
hating every moment.

A lot of my friends went abroad on holiday, but in 1998 my
dad had borrowed a caravan in Clacton, Essex, so my brother
and I had been allowed to miss school during Events Week
(the penultimate week of the year) to go. Now, I had to fill the
upcoming six blank weeks as best I could. The trouble is,
having total free rein over what you can do after a whole school
year of being told exactly what to do for every minute of every
day is really difficult. No one ever teaches you how to relax –
there are never any lessons on how to fill your free time.

I couldn't relax anyway because I had so much to think
about – namely the biggest crush I had ever encountered:
Michael. I had no idea how to articulate how I felt about him.
Pop music of the time had nothing to offer except 'Save
Tonight' by Eagle-Eye Cherry and I knew Michael probably

wasn't going to save tonight or any night for me. He had a big smile (and braces) and played the flute in the school orchestra but was still respected enough by the boys to play football with them. I couldn't imagine having the confidence to bestride both these worlds and still make time to smile. In fact, I could not fathom how such a perfect, magnetic person could even exist.

It transcended lust – it was more than that, I just wanted him to be part of my life. Rather than anything lewd, my fantasy life with him involved living in a bungalow (the stately home had gone out of the window already), sharing the housework and planning trips to the seaside – he'd understand everything about me without me having to explain a thing. Typically for me, even my fantasies were more like the pages of *Saga Magazine* – at fifteen, I basically wanted to retire.

I also knew that even though I loved my family, I would gladly leave them all for *dead* if it meant spending the rest of my life with him.

An idea planted itself in my head during those long summer days. I would phone him at home! This was in the days when mobile phones barely existed (except if you were that girl in the year below whose dad bought her one to make himself feel better about the affair he was having behind her mum's back that everyone knew about except her). I would ask Michael if he was free to do something – not a date, obviously, just an afternoon of whatever he wanted, really. I dialled the number, waited. His mum picked up the phone.

Throughout most of my teenage years I was much more interested in getting along with my friends' mums than I was with them. We just had so much more in common – coffee mornings, what to make for tea, getting stuff organised for food tech. Michael's mum liked me, I could tell. '. . . Anyway, Tom, I'll let you know what roller blinds I end up going with – hang on a second now, Michael's just here . . .'

A horrible moment followed as I waited for Michael to come to the phone. '. . . Ah, yello,' he said, like he was an estate agent trying to seem chipper but at the same time too busy to say 'hello' properly. I usually hate it when teenagers try to act like they're fully fledged grown-ups before their time (even though this is exactly what I'd been doing since I was seven).

'Michael, hey! It's Tom . . .'

There was a momentary pause. 'Oh, all right?'

'Yeah! Yeah, just fine, thanks. You?'

'Yeah, yeah, good, my cousins are round . . .'

Of course he'd have cousins to keep him company! He wasn't like me with no cousins and no friends because he was too scared of being taken to a gangland Laser Quest. What was I thinking? And how selfish of me to invade his precious cousin-time.

'Oh, that's nice. I was just wondering—'

'Yeah? . . . I'll be there in a sec!' he shouted out. Those cousins were clearly impatient.

'I, er, was just wondering if you fancied hanging out or doing something?'

'I can't my cousins are round.' He was really into these cousins.

'No! Not now, now-now, haha! Maybe, like, over the weekend?'

'Nah, I can't – my cousins are round.' I was not comprehending the importance of the cousins. 'Anyway, I've gotta go. Later.'

'OK. Nice to ta—' he'd gone. If his mum knew he'd spoken to me like that, she would have been furious – she liked me!

At this time, in my extremely naïve worldview, I actually thought there were plenty of young couples who had got together because 'Well, we were just having such a great time chatting with my mum that I just knew we were going to shag and be together, forever.'

If I was honest, I could never see myself acting on fancying Michael, but I still crushed hard on him – I couldn't comprehend that us being together was anything other than inevitable. Despite him clearly being heterosexual and/or not interested in me. It's only as an adult I've come to realise why they're called crushes; I had assumed it was something to do with a juice or maybe velvet (even then I brought everything back to soft furnishings), but they're called crushes because they crush every part of you and you can barely think or move because the crush is weighing you down. Now I was *crushed* not only by Michael but also by the memory of that terrible phone call. A phone call I couldn't even talk to anyone about.

This ongoing heartache situation had to stop – I'd had enough. No more moping around in the summer holidays when I should be, as my mother said, 'Out there, enjoying the beautiful sunshine!' I didn't really want to be out there, enjoying the sunshine at the best of times. What I really wanted was a purpose.

The mid-to-late nineties were a drab time. Television consisted of Nicholas Witchell reporting on the news and shows like *This Life* (why was their flat so dark? Why was she so angry about being a lawyer – surely, that's a good job?) and *Silent Witness* (where the main character was a corpse). And having any kind of hobby or even enthusiasm for something felt very exposing – like people would laugh at me: 'Oh my God-da! How sad! He collects stamps and is happy with himself!'

The closest thing I had to a hobby was cooking. I loved it. I think because it combined my two favourite things, which were eating and showing off. My favourite GCSE subject was, without question, food technology. I would have done just plain old 'cooking' if I'd been given half a chance, but it had to be framed as a 'technology' – as though it had to be made practical, less flamboyant, more masculine. The other options included graphics, which everyone seemed to do but I didn't like because it meant carrying a big plastic red-handled briefcase which bashed into your knees. It was assumed by my dad that I would do the third option, electronics, because it was deemed more academic and also my dad had been an electrician at one point.

Food tech did involve me making things like a chicken fricassee and also, for one very long project, a sandwich. More than this, it meant I could hang out with all the bad girls (called this because they were very confident and rude to all the teachers), who all seemed to have chosen food technology as well. They had blow waves in their hair and carried their school bags like handbags high up on their shoulders and in doing so looked like fifteen-year-old middle-aged women. I wanted to be just like them. In fact, one of them got engaged to her boyfriend because they were too young to actually get married. They'd been together for two years, which was unheard of. Apparently they'd got engaged while sharing a bath. To me, this was like hearing about another planet, as the thought of me getting engaged while sharing a bath with someone in my family home while my parents were sat downstairs watching

Only Fools and Horses and eating toast would always be unthinkable.

Everyone was scared of the bad girls because if anyone was ever rude back to them, they'd have no hesitation in saying, 'You wanna shut your maaaaaafffff, or I'll get my cousins to come down to beat the shit out of you!' Some people really loved their cousins. Mine all lived in Australia.

Year 10 food technology was based around a project on sandwiches, except our teacher pronounced sandwiches as 'Sang-wiches'. 'Get out your sangwich projects please, Year 10,' she'd shout across the model kitchen, and all the bad girls would laugh, and to be like them, so would I.

The sangwich project was housed in a ring binder as big as my chest and included pages of boring bar graphs displaying the results of 'surveys' where we'd asked our families binary questions like 'If you were buying a sandwich would you choose chicken or ham?' (Being a vegetarian was unheard of). The bad girls had much more varied results as they had all those cousins to ask. I only had my mum, dad and my brother to ask, and I already knew they preferred ham because that was what we had in the fridge. It was wafer thin and we regarded it as quite a delicacy.

However, the subject had lit a touchpaper for my love of cooking. Our teacher was a tall woman with long, pleated skirts, a patent handbag and immaculately coiffed hair on top of her head. Once, when I mentioned how I'd been watching Delia Smith's *Autumn Collection,* her face literally lit up.

I loved tapping her up for food-preparation intel. For example, how you should use a milk glaze on savoury pies and an egg glaze on sweet pies so you can always tell the difference when they're waiting to be cooked. She'd also slip in opinions along the way, which was quite unnerving. 'Your chicken fric-assee needs more parsley, and I think Jimmy Tarbuck is the entertainer of his generation.' And then she'd move away very quickly but smoothly, like she was on casters.

Not having any friends during the summer holidays meant I was very much reliant on the social calendar of my parents. Mum hated having people round because of several insecurities about the house, such as the taps in the downstairs toilet, which had not been replaced since the house was built in the 1960s. All the neighbours had 'vanity units' and Victorian-style brass taps, which seemed so much more fabulous. This reticence from Mum meant I had to wait for their friends to invite us (them and, therefore, *me*) round.

One Sunday, we were going to Wendy and Daryl's. 'Oh no, you're not going to come out dressed like that, are you? Can't you wear something normal?' decried Mum as I descended the stairs in my favourite double-breasted blazer with brassy buttons and a nice tie, which seemed perfectly normal for me as a fifteen-year-old going to a barbecue with his parents.

'Come on, for gawd's sake! I said we'd be there by now!' Dad interrupted. Dad is always punctual and thus frustrated as my mum continues to be late for everything. At this moment, she was spraying Yves Saint Laurent Rive Gauche from a very glamorous blue-and-black cylindrical receptacle and grabbing a bottle of nail varnish to paint her nails in the car on the way there. 'It's not a fancy do! No one's going to be dressed up – wear that nice T-shirt I bought you for your birthday, please . . . Go on, do it for your mum.'

Mum and I were intimidated by Wendy and Daryl and their elaborate barbecues – they seemed to have such strong opinions on everything, from the assassination of JFK to the collapse of the ruble to the best way to barbecue a chicken. To gain a sense of control of the situation, Mum and I swapped the first letters of their names around so we felt less fearful sat there, in Dendy and Waryl's lounge where everyone was assembled, smoking.

All of their friends smoked cigarettes constantly and very glamorously. The brand was St Moritz and came in a dark-green square box with a gold trim. The cigarettes themselves even had a gold band round them and a clear filter. They were placed in immaculately manicured hands with long bright-red nails, held on high and used for occasional gesticulating, before being drawn down to bright-red lips as punctuation to many opinions.

'Should we worry about passive smoking? They say that's bad?' I'd ask needily.

'*Shut. Up,*' Dad would bark back, already frustrated at being made late for his friends.

Their house had white painted walls, not patterned ones like the Laura Ashley wallpapered walls we had. We didn't know you were allowed to go so simple with interiors. At Dendy and Waryl's, bright prints full of reds and blues adorned the walls alongside cabinets of Daryl's tennis trophies (Dad said Daryl was the best tennis player he had ever met. Daryl also had a moustache and a tendency to wear tennis shorts on social occasions, which even I felt was too much. He also had a great love of Phil Collins).

An actual whole salmon, barbecued chicken legs and salads were served on beautiful platters – massive white plates with pink, blue and orange fruits painted on them. The chicken had herbs – *real* herbs, not the dried 'mixed herbs' we had at the back of the cupboard. They actually had garlic in the house, which they cooked with the chicken, and Mum and Dad didn't complain about it like when I used one clove in my famous chicken fricassee.

Conversation was always 'to the point' and always based on Dendy and Waryl's celebrated opinions – there wasn't time for 'feelings'. I found this out quite abruptly when asked by Wendy 'How are you feeling, Tom? Are you happy at school?'.

I replied, 'I like my school work but sometimes I feel a bit you know . . . depressed.'

'Depressed? Depressed?! *Depressed?!* What have you got to be depressed about? You've got a dad, haven't you?' and she inhaled another breath of her cigarette emphatically.

I quickly learnt that I should have replied with, 'Yes, I'm fine, thanks,' and left it at that.

On one occasion, religion entered the fray as one of their friends announced, 'Well, Catholics don't believe in Jesus, do they?' – her cigarette brought down for a brief inhale – 'They just believe in Mary.'

Everyone nodded and took a puff in solemn agreement, the tobacco smoke like the incense wafted around by Catholic priests. Mum and I knew this to be absolute rubbish, mainly because my grandmother was a Catholic who loved to bring out a statue of him at Christmas and also I was doing religious education at GCSE.

I had a really nice RE teacher who talked about everything and was the first person who told us that Section 28 existed and that she wasn't allowed to say it was OK to be gay. But she still did. Her name was Ms Jamieson and she was awesome.

Wendy's sermon of nonsense made me realise something – if you deliver an opinion with enough confidence alongside the most fabulous barbecue in suburbia and finish it off with the old-world sophistication of a waved-around cigarette, everyone will put you at the centre of their social circle.

And that's when I realised what my focus – my plan – would be for this summer holiday; I would make myself the centre of my social circle: I would be my very own Wendy.

If I could throw a dinner party, I might finally be respected. I'd have so many friends I'd get to complain about how busy I was – the luxury of being socially exhausted. Most importantly, I'd be someone Michael would love to hang out with. He and I would spend forever talking to each other about our thoughts and feelings. We'd possibly be sat on a picnic blanket near the sea and I would be talking, smiling – even listening to him drone on about his feelings – while also stoically processing the fact that I'd recently left my entire family for dead.

Perhaps it could be considered unusual for a fifteen-year-old boy to decide he'd emulate a forty-seven-year-old woman because of her lovely nails and garish plate collection, but I had no idea as I was too busy to even think about it. One thing I did know was that somehow this plan would have to be kept secret – people might laugh at me, and also I could never let other people know about my Michael obsession.

With nothing to do now that the holidays had begun, I was able to dedicate all of my time to working out the best course of action. To make my dinner party special, I had to rely on what I already had in my armoury: proficient cooking based on one year of food tech and my GCSE Sandwich Project; an obsession with the programme *Ready Steady Cook*; a growing reputation for being a little eccentric; and a propensity for making things overtly formal.

A trip to Bromley Central Library was in order as I needed to learn how to do things properly. Nothing was to be left to chance – I needed to master the one tool that middle-class housewives and gays have been using since time immemorial to bolster their superiority: correct social etiquette.

The library had a copy of Emily Post's *Etiquette: The Blue Book of Social Usage*. At over seven hundred pages, this tome from 1922 was exactly what I needed to make my social standing stand out combined with my weekend penchant for folding napkins.

Published in America as a guide for the newly emerging aspirational middle classes, it was designed to provide the lady of the house with advice on how to dress her butler, how to arrange claret glasses and how it's impolite to thank the servants for every dish served (it interrupts their work when they then feel obliged to constantly say, 'You're welcome, ma'am,' in return).

I was obsessed with learning all of it. What I had failed to consider was that I was not the wealthy lady of a grand house in America in 1922 but a fifteen-year-old boy earning three pounds per dog walk and living in Bromley in his parents' house. But at this stage it didn't matter because I just had to do all I could to show how superior I was. Surely, my knowledge of different types of soup spoons would make Michael want to ditch his cousins to spend time with me?

It is a truth universally acknowledged that a homosexual teenager will sublimate his sexual fantasies into an obsession with tableware. A gift came in the form of a small responsibility. Briony and George, mum and dad's friends round the corner were going abroad on one of their cultural visits (they had actual papyrus pictures of pharaohs framed on their wall from when they went to the actual pyramids, in Egypt – not the mocked up version I had so enjoyed at Chessington World of Adventures). They were the epitome of post-war social mobility, and I knew Briony loved throwing dinner parties.

While they were going on one of their trips, they needed someone to clear the post from their front doormat so that would-be burglars wouldn't realise their treasure-trove house was empty. They foolishly gave me a key to their front door and the job of collecting the numerous letters and *National Geographics* from the mat and putting them on the dining table and turning on some lamps to make it look like someone was there. It was always a small lamp at the back of the house, suggesting the occupant cowered in a corner at the back with their travel magazines. Everyone in our area was totally convinced they were going to be burgled at any time which, in a way, was kind of presumptuous given some of their curtains.

The letter-clearing and lamp-putting-on was a job any idiot could have done as it took no time at all. So I used that time, that ill-gotten freedom I had in their house, to abuse their trust and do the unthinkable: I went through their tableware dresser.

With gay abandon – literally – I flung open the cupboards and drawers and looked at all the plates and cutlery they had: shiny silver-plated knives and forks, soup spoons and fish knives all arranged immaculately in a mahogany canteen and beautiful blue-rimmed china in so many shapes and sizes. Something for every possible course. And, oh, the courses that Briony must have been able to serve! Emily Post herself would have been delighted (Emily Post believed seven courses is the bare minimum for any dinner party).

I couldn't contain my excitement and started to get the china and the cutlery out onto the table, arranging it just like Emily Post had instructed me to. It was so exciting to see everything arranged as it should be! This was long before I could have taken a photo on a phone to gaze upon at my leisure or even researched on Pinterest to see other examples of elegant table settings to compare it to. This wasn't some sort of perverted sexual encounter I describe – it was just something I needed to do. Though it certainly did give new meaning to the phrase 'lay the table'.

If daytime detective dramas have taught us anything, it's that a criminal will always make one fatal mistake. My mistake was complacency. As I was exploring options for where to best place a soup tureen I looked round to see, standing before me, Clive, Briony and George's neighbour, clutching a badminton racket.

This was no time for a game – apart from anything else china is notoriously breakable. 'Oh thank gawd! I thought they'd been burgled,' he cried. I realised my mistake instantly. The sight of the door ajar and the hall light must have given the game away – no one would read their travel magazines at the front of the house and certainly not in the hallway. '. . . But it's just you. Thank God, they haven't been broken into.'

Poor Clive, if only he'd known they *had* been broken into! Their sideboard had been absolutely ransacked! What had become of me? I wondered what he thought he was going to do with a badminton racket, the swooshiest of all the sports weapons, had he come across a band of burglars.

Clive glanced at the avalanche of tableware behind me, but I think the adrenaline of the situation meant he couldn't process why this fifteen-year-old had decided to host an imaginary dinner party, so he left without saying anything. In Bromley, if saying nothing is an option, that's what people will always do.

Back on home territory, I became very busy practising and getting out the cutlery that my mum had bought with her staff discount at The Army & Navy. It only usually came out on Christmas Day and actually even that had stopped as Dad said he didn't like the shape of the forks in his hand. There was also some white china, which was a wedding present for my parents back in 1972, that hadn't been used since Mum and Dad invited a solicitor round to update their wills. Social occasions for my parents seemed to be tempered with choking on opinions and cigarette smoke or making plans for inevitable death.

Two things were still missing: a dress rehearsal and any guests coming to the aforementioned dinner party. At this rate I was going to be throwing an elaborate meal for me and our two Yorkshire terriers, who were my main companions during these long summer days. I needed to invite some human friends.

A guest list had to be drawn up in order to lure Michael round. We had friends in common – Jo was one of my best friends and we'd helped each other with revising Jane Austen and asexual plants. Also Jo's brother James could come too, as he knew Michael from football.

I also decided that this should be a lunch party and not a dinner party because that meant my parents would be at work and I'd have the house to myself. My younger brother was out all the time because he was either playing sports (which, I've mentioned, he was naturally good at) or round at the house of one of his friends (which, as we also know, he was naturally good at making). An evening dinner party would involve Mum being at home, getting anxious that I'd kill myself with the blender. If Dad was home, I'd feel self-conscious about making fancy food – even now he can sometimes regard using serving dishes as an affectation.

More guests were required for this 'luncheon' (as Emily Post taught me to say, because 'lunch' is an abbreviation and therefore 'common') and I knew exactly who else to invite: the flamboyant and wonderful Brigitte, another of my best friends, who wore fabulous dresses and was a natural performer. We'd become friends because we both did drama and I'd make her perform scenes from Noël Coward plays with me.

Jo, James and Brigitte all said yes – after half an hour chatting to their mums, I briefly asked my school friends if they wanted to come and they said, 'Yeah, sure' – this didn't reflect the importance of the moment at all. Now it was my moment to invite Michael. The same racing heartbeat in my chest. I spoke to his mum, who was always so positive about me, and she thought it was an excellent idea that I was throwing a lunch. 'A luncheon,' I corrected. She laughed – we really could be best friends.

Michael was bored because he hadn't been out of the house for days. Perfect! He was delighted to accept the invitation. Luncheon – next Thursday. It was currently Wednesday. So there were eight days to go. A party of five for lunch. It was an odd number, but it would have to do.

Now I needed to practise being my very own Wendy and what better way to prepare than by actually inviting *the* Wendy round for a dry run. I mentioned to Dad I wanted to practise my cooking during the holidays and to invite Wendy and Daryl for dinner. Dad, delighted that I was actually doing something with my time, immediately phoned them. Unfortunately, Daryl was unable to come as he had a tennis tournament scheduled for that day. I didn't care as I was not remotely interested in him – it was Wendy's opinion I coveted. Wendy was available. That Friday. She'd be there.

I knew what I was doing when I spoke to my dad about it on the sly. As soon as Mum was told panic ensued. 'What?!

Tomorrow? I'll have to hoover the house, and I haven't got any food in, and will Wendy need to smoke in the house? I hate the smell of smoke in the house! But it'll need to be a clean house for her to smoke in. Oh, gawd, the downstairs toilet – I'll have to repaint it!'

In television programmes, people seem to have visitors round all the time and there's no panic. In soap operas like *Neighbours,* everyone is constantly wandering into one another's homes – sometimes without even knocking – and there's no fanfare about it. In fact, sometimes they walk in and help themselves to orange juice straight from the fridge. My friend Marianne from across the road did this once and Mum was aghast. I was discouraged from having friends round again.

In cookery programmes, the chefs are always keen to say how 'a few friends just popped round for a light bite and it was no trouble to just whip up a quick fish pie'. Not for the Allen family – there was never any 'just' about it – *just* stress. If anyone came round, it had to be planned months in advance and worried about constantly.

Television chefs have nothing to worry about because they're often a bit like those posh, confident people (confidence and being posh often go hand in hand, I find) who don't seem to worry about anything. The posh-confident don't have shame in their imperfections and untidy houses because they don't need to care what other people think – they're already the centre of their social world simply because they're so posh-confident. They revel in their odd chairs, mismatching plates, dirty sink and the cat having licked the bread that is about to be served to the guests.

'Come as you are!', 'Take me as I am!' are the opposite of what my family believe. 'Come as you aren't' would be more apt. '*Mi casa es su casa*' – no, it isn't. This *casa* is mine – *Su* should stay in her own *casa*.

The candles were still burning, the meal was over and Wendy put her dessert spoon down and reached for her cigarettes. Taking one out of the gold-trimmed box, she put it to her mouth. Then she waited, staring at me with her eyebrows raised.

'Well?' she said.

'Well, what?'

'Don't you know a gentleman should always light a cigarette for a lady?'

I did not know this. Also, because my mum has always been terrified of the house catching fire and all of us burning to death, I was never allowed to light a match, never mind use a cigarette lighter. Panic often brings out the best in me and after two attempts I somehow nervously lit it and Wendy violently brought her cigarette to the flame.

'Do you want my honest opinion?'

'Yes?' I said, tentatively, stroking one of the Yorkshire terriers as a support dog. Mum and Dad sat on the opposite side of the table, quaking in Wendy's judgement of their eldest son. This was a huge day for them.

'The starter? The rolled fish in the beurre blanc? Excellent.' She said, 'excellent' emphatically with a sharp, flat movement of her manicured hand, like she was underlining her strong opinion in mid-air.

Mum and Dad's faces lit up.

'Then the chicken fricassee? . . . Ordinary. I mean, it's fine, but nothing special. I could do that myself, mid-week, no bother.' I knew I should have put more parsley in it. 'The fish, though? *Excellent.*'

'And the dessert?' I asked. 'The chocolate ganache on a chocolate crumb, moulded into a cylindrical shape?'

'That was excellent. I'd pay for that.' She drew a sharp intake of smoke and blew it upwards to show that this was her final judgement, grey tendrils ascending like she was signifying a new pope.

I knew pudding would be a success because I'd got it off a free recipe card with my subscription to the *Ready Steady Cook* magazine that my dad had got me. The first edition included a ring binder, and I was very proud of it.

'What I would say though,' said Wendy, taking another long inhale, 'the fish would be nicer if you had fish knives and forks. Makes it proper. You want it to be proper, don't you?'

'Yes, of course!' I said, the other Yorkshire terrier coming over now for a share of the attention.

'How old are those dogs?' asked Wendy, changing the subject.

'Eleven!' I said, almost proffering them up as a final course in the meal.

'That breed,' she pointed at the dogs with her cigarette, 'rarely make it past twelve. Enjoy them while they're around they could be dead in a year.' Another sharp intake of smoke and a puff out to show this was the last note on the matter.

Troubling dog-morbidity chat aside, I knew that she was right about the fish knives. The next morning I went to The Army & Navy with the remnants of my birthday money (approximately thirty-seven pounds) and headed to the table-ware section with its bright spotlights designed to show the gleaming plates and forks.

I perused the cutlery in a cautious manner. Even then, a teenager purchasing knives, albeit unusual table ones, could arouse the suspicion that maybe I was going to use them for violence. Though what sort of effete gang they imagined me joining, I can only imagine.

'Tom?' I turned round abruptly, not used to having anyone say my name because I hadn't spoken to anybody for some time and our Yorkshire terriers couldn't talk. It was my Religious Education teacher. 'Tom, what are you doing here? Buying tableware?' she asked, laughing, even though I didn't think there was anything remotely funny about buying tableware.

'No, actually I'm throwing a luncheon on Thursday.'

'Oh my! A luncheon, eh?' she said, still laughing. It was like no one else in the world had read Emily Post except me.

'. . . So, you know, I needed to buy some fish knives.'

'Oh, of course you did!'

'Would you like to come?' I said, suddenly realising I had that spare place at the table to make it up to a six. What could be more impressive to Michael? Not only could I command the social whirl of my peer group but the teachers as well.

'Oh, how kind! What a lovely . . . but . . . err . . .' She floundered, searching desperately for an excuse. 'Well, I'd be absolutely delighted!'

It was settled. The perfect six. A closeted fifteen-year-old possessed by the character Hyacinth Bucket, his RE teacher, his two school friends, a random brother, two potentially dead Yorkshire terriers and the crush of his life all coming round for the perfect meal.

The table was set the day before. 'You're going to get all of this out, are you?' asked Mum, accusingly. There's no reference in films of a teenager behaving like this and I felt guilty about it – slamming doors and bunking off school would have been much easier for them to deal with.

The next morning, the house to myself, I was up early making a chocolate ganache mousse, a sauce for fish and a chicken fricassee. The napkins had been folded and the wine glasses polished, even though we weren't having wine because we were still children.

Ready at twelve thirty in my blazer with the brassy buttons, I jumped as the doorbell rang. It was Jo and her brother. Next up my RE teacher, who was very happy to be there and her presence added to the excitement of the afternoon. Jo's brother stared awkwardly at her in silence. But where was Michael? A car pulled up outside. His mum dropping him off with a bottle of Schloer non-alcoholic fizz – clearly a suggestion from my best friend, his mum. Getting out of the same car was Brigitte. The dogs started yapping incessantly. I was so embarrassed.

'Come on in! Lovely to see you! Thanks so much for coming!' I was doing so well at being the perfect host. I felt just like Wendy, but without the smoke and the opinions. Michael looked bewildered.

'Come and sit at the table, everyone – luncheon is served!' Everyone came to sit down while I went to present the first course ('starter' is not a word Emily Post cared for). I was excited – I was getting to spend time with Michael! The food looked perfect and when I brought it out, I was a little angry that no one had placed their napkins on their laps. 'Napkins on laps, everyone!' I said, laughing but in a passive-aggressive way.

Jo and her brother started laughing because they could see I was taking it so seriously. Brigitte then did a flamboyant display of tucking her napkin down her beautiful dress and Michael immediately laughed and so did the RE teacher. Was everyone laughing at me or with me? It didn't matter – I was content to be spending time with Michael.

Despite no one knowing how to use fish knives and Michael even saying at one point, 'What's these then?' (I could forgive him, since it was Michael) the meal was a triumph and we all laughed and I think even Emily Post herself would have been proud. Our RE teacher said if this was a coursework project, it would get an A★, which was strange because it wasn't in any way a religious meal, except for perhaps a passing connection between Jesus feeding the five thousand with loaves and fishes and my recently purchased fish knives. Deluded as I was, even I would struggle to compare my kitchen niftiness to the Son of God.

Just as I felt it all could not have gone any better, it all went so wrong. Jo was giggling. 'Michael – don't you and Brigitte want to tell us something?'

'*Nooooo* . . .' Brigitte responded, giggling. Even the RE teacher was giggling.

Jo just decided to say it anyway. 'You and Michael are going out now, aren't you?!'

They both laughed. Everyone laughed with silly teenage joy at the news. Except me. I laughed with fake joy – fish knife through heart, heartbreak fake joy. All this work, all this anguish and cutlery and now to be humiliated in front of my RE teacher and the boy of my dreams. To think, I'd folded napkins especially. Of course, it wasn't their fault, I'd never told them how I felt – I'd never felt confident enough to tell them anything – but somehow, in my fantasy, I'd expected them to know and for it to somehow all work out.

To top it all off, the dogs started trying to mount each other in front of everyone in the middle of the lounge carpet – Emily Post hated the word 'lounge' but by now it didn't matter what she thought. Even the dogs were mocking me. Michael and everyone thought it was hilarious and even more hilarious because I was so red-faced. They had all had a wonderful time. They loved it all. They were so grateful that I'd organised it. In truth, I had wasted my summer holidays organising the perfect date for Michael and somebody else.

It was over – the meal, the fantasy, everything. Our RE teacher said she was honoured to have been invited and got in her Rover and left. Jo offered to help me with the washing up, but I declined – I was just glad of something to do, something to distract me from what had happened.

As they drove off, I saw the look on Michael's mum's face. My best mum-friend was laughing. How could she?

I felt so foolish to think cooking could ever change the path of my little life in the corner of suburbia. Washing up the endless dishes – the mess I'd made for myself – as hurriedly as possible so the house would be back to normal for when Mum got off her bus. Now I was stuck with a collection of unnecessary fish knives and a rule book of etiquette that had to be returned to the library and which no one even cared about anyway.

Of course, I was happy for them – they were my friends, and if he was going to be with anyone, I was glad it was the fabulous Brigitte. I'd just got distracted by a chicken fricassee, thinking it would make everything OK – not for the last time. Not knowing how to be a teenager, I'd reached out to the only guide I could find, an etiquette book from 1922, and cheated life itself by leap-frogging over the teenage years to become the middle-aged suburban housewife I'd always wanted to be. It turned out that it wasn't everything I dreamed, far from it in fact, but at least I had found something to fill those long empty days of summer.

4

Dressing

When I was sixteen, I dressed in Victorian clothing in a bid to distract people from the fact that I was gay. It was a flawed plan.

I once said this during an interview on television in Australia. '. . . To *distract* people from being gay?! How did that work? Surely this would have made you stick out more?!' asked the presenter, pulling a face to the camera. I've always had to explain myself. Some people can only see things in straight lines.

By Victorian clothing I mean I liked to wear bow ties, starched detachable wing collars, double-breasted waistcoats, tailcoats and, left to my own devices, a bowler hat. On one occasion I saw a teacher as I was getting on a train and I said hello to him; he literally pretended he didn't know me and ran to the next carriage. My teachers were embarrassed to see me, when it should have been the other way around – that's how weird I was.

In a way, I was pleased. I wasn't really dressing in Victorian clothing to distract from me being gay or me being anything. I dressed in outlandish period clothing to try to be someone else altogether – preferably someone from a different era, perversely even if that era was a lot more restrictive. Just as long as it was a long time away from me in the here and now. Despite being rational in all other aspects of my life I was convinced that if I wore clothing from a different century and believed hard enough that I was someone else I could actually even travel through time.

It may seem strange, but I believed it would be easier if I could be someone else, living in a different world. That way I could avoid all the awkward truths that had come to the surface about myself; I could be in a world where I didn't have to expend my energy on secret longings for boys at school. If only I could amputate these awkward truths altogether I'd be free, though free to pursue what exactly, I had no idea.

I've always found it hard to explain eloquently – no one is given a manual on themselves to put in the glove box of their life for use during a breakdown – but I just didn't have a very clear understanding of myself. Having felt that I was different from an early age caused a discord between myself and the world around me, and with nowhere to express it outwardly, this discord did a U-turn back at me. It produced a self-loathing so profound and insidious that even I wasn't aware of it. All I knew was that I wanted to be different to what I was.

The other thing about romanticising past eras is that they feel safe when you look back because we know in retrospect what's going to happen next. It's not as though back in 1944 people were saying, 'OK, just one more year and we'll have got this war out of the way.'

In my personal fantasy of living in the 1800s, I wasn't worried about the poverty, the miserable working conditions or the fact that at some point I'd be marched off to fight in some war. It didn't seem to cross my mind that back then it would have been absolutely horrendous to be gay or even a little different. In my mind, I would have been the exception because I'd be so busy starching collars.

As this time travel was apparently impossible and with no road map for how I was supposed to go forward, I decided to get lost in the biggest fantasy of them all – the movies. I taped things from TV to use as my guidebook: *Remains of the Day,* about inter-war servants who prioritised their jobs to deny their feelings; *Mary Poppins,* about a bowler-hatted George Banks who was disconnected from his family because he denied his feelings; *Top Hat* with Fred Astaire and clothes so immaculate he had to dance instead of having actual feelings.

I also liked films about powerful people who were accompanied by high ceremony, so they didn't seem to have feelings either: *The Madness of King George*, *Flash Gordon* and *The Last Emperor.* In fact, for a long time when I was around four or five I didn't have any friends because I told the other children that I *was* an emperor. I would frequently sit at the top of the stairs in a dressing gown with a tea cosy on my head and I felt very regal, as I'm sure you can imagine. The other children, as usual, did not want to play along.

I actually hated Flash Gordon, but I loved his arch-nemesis, Ming – he had the best clothes with high collars and all he did was swish around in a big red cloak and walk down stairs dramatically, ordering people be executed. So much more interesting than stupid Flash Gordon, standing there in his pants with long hair, making a mess of the furniture and telling people to love each other.

I used to think that loving the baddies in films and TV shows meant yet another thing must be wrong with me – was I fundamentally evil? Now I realise I like them so much because the baddies get the best lines and the best outfits. More than that, they also get to have power over their circumstances. No one makes them feel silly or tells them to 'Shhh!'. Instead, everyone has to bow and curtsey to them to make them feel the opposite of silly. Until the last act of the film, they control everything in their world. They wage wars and foil enemies and command things, and they don't have to worry about being accepted because everyone wants to be accepted by them.

I also seemed to like things to do with aliens, I guess because I felt like one at times, so I really loved the film *Independence Day* and the TV series *The X Files*. Though I think this may also have been due to having a crush on David Duchovny and Gillian Anderson's shoulder pads.

Despite feeling so awkward and such an outsider, there were nice people in my year group at school who'd invite me to their house parties. As we progressed up the years, I found people weren't as judgemental because they now had new focuses — namely, themselves and how they were regarded by the people they fancied. These gatherings would normally involve going round to someone's house because their mum had gone on some sort of minibreak.

Girls would put on tight dresses that had no shoulder straps and would curl their hair so a strand or two would come down over their face. They'd bring bottles of cheap white wine and Lambrini bought in off-licences without being asked for ID because they looked like adults now. Sometimes, they'd bring bottles of alcopops (which had just been invented) and were basically fizzy orange with booze in them. They caused a tabloid backlash because they might encourage teenagers to drink (which they did) and cause the death of civilisation (which they didn't — that was Pot Noodle).

Sometimes the girls would drink beer because this was also the age of the 'ladette'. I never really understood what this meant other than teenage girls drinking beer. I knew that I was as far from being a 'lad' as possible and thus even more unfashionable. Everything felt a bit like a documentary I was watching on the TV but wasn't a part of.

Boys would wear Ralph Lauren shirts, which were untucked from their jeans, and white trainers. Hair was gelled down flat to the top of their head, and maybe the occasional ear piercing could be seen. Boys also arrived with blue off-licence bags filled with cans of beer that they slammed down on the kitchen counter like magnanimous bon vivants, but rather than speaking like bon vivants, they just went 'Aaaahhhhh!' in a playful way that I felt was still aggressive.

I never knew how to go about acquiring alcohol as I was too scared to go to the off-licence – I didn't have a fake ID, despite being good at crafts and laminating, and besides, if the shopkeeper had asked for one I think I would have run away embarrassed. The teenage boys and girls I'd grown up with didn't worry. They didn't worry about anything. Suddenly they seemed to be like actual adults, learning to drive and earning money from weekend jobs while busily 'getting off' with each other – which only meant kissing (though since I wasn't part of this world, I may have misunderstood and maybe it did mean actual sex).

What was clear was even though I often dressed as an adult in a three-piece suit and matching pocket square, I was not ready for this at all. I only went to these parties because somehow I thought I should – this was the sort of thing teenagers were supposed to be doing and the alternative was sitting at home feeling miserable, so I felt I may as well go out and feel

miserable, and maybe something would shift or I'd learn something about myself.

In truth, I would have been much happier staying at home
as it would have given me the chance to finally clear out my
sock drawer, go through my postcard collection or give the
bathroom a once over, all while keeping an eye on my parents.
There was absolutely no need to keep an eye on them, I just
felt somehow like I should be there to protect them – from
what, I didn't know, and how I would protect them, I had no
idea – I could barely look after myself!

I'd reluctantly tell Mum and Dad I'd been invited to a party
and Dad would immediately offer to give me a lift because he
prides himself on always giving lifts. Dad would also suggest I
take some of his beers so I didn't go empty-handed. I agreed,
even though I really didn't like beer. We would pull up to the
house party and I'd immediately ask Dad to come and pick me
up.

'Sure, Tom, when shall I come back?'

'In half an hour?'

'You sure?!' I'd reassure Dad that was more than long enough
for me to see the people I wanted to see, be a totally normal
teenager and then get home to watch *Gardeners' World* on
BBC2.

Walking in, the party would be dark and loud and smell of
cheap aftershave and cigarette smoke. Never knowing what I
was supposed to do or who I should talk to, I'd head straight to
the kitchen. I did have some friends at this point and sometimes I'd spend time catching up with them, but I was aware
that my (usually female) friends had ambitions to get off with
boys. Especially if some of the – terrifying to me – boys from
a neighbouring school had been invited.

Not wanting to stand in the way of true love, I'd hang back in the kitchen, looking at the spice rack. I'd maybe try to look casual while waiting for an opportune moment to start a conversation with someone, lolling against the work surface before realising it had made my elbow soaking wet. I'd look at the soggy counter where plastic bags were now swimming in spilled wine and beer and think how disappointing this idea of a party was – such a missed opportunity by the host to put out canapés and crisps (the only form of 'putting out' I was familiar with at this time).

The truth is, the host was probably a bottle of wine deep, swinging from her mum's rotary washing line with her heavily applied eye make-up streaming down her face as she wept because that boy from Eltham College she fancied was getting off with her best friend.

This was not a world I wanted to be part of. I looked down my nose at them, but as with all snobbery, it was really just fear in disguise. I was totally terrified of this world where getting drunk risked showing your feelings, and I was absolutely ashamed of having any feelings at all, never mind gay ones.

Not knowing what else to do at the parties and not fitting in with either the girls or the boys, I decided I needed a purpose, so I'd find a black bin-liner and start clearing up (even if they were on a minibreak, I was determined to make a good impression on everyone's mum and make more mum-friends).

I'd also find a cloth and wipe up any sticky surfaces, which more often than not had an arse pressed against them while two of my classmates started 'getting off' with each other. 'Don't mind me,' I'd passive-aggressively mutter as I wiped around them – more concerned for the water marks left on the Formica than any awkwardness about getting in the way of my friends' face-eating.

It felt like my version of rebelling – I was doing the exact opposite of what I was expected to do. Somehow I felt like I was exercising some sort of control over my life, however perversely. When my 'party cleaning' was done, I'd quietly slip out of the door and into Dad's car.

'Did you have a nice time then?' Dad would say, looking up from the Jeffrey Archer book he'd been reading while I was inside. 'Oh, marvellous,' I'd say, as we sped home for me to catch up on Alan Titchmarsh.

At the approach of the new millennium, it felt like things weren't particularly progressive: ladette culture was matched by lad culture where teenage boys were encouraged to read magazines like FHM talking about tits and football and options on how to wear a tracksuit. I was more interested in reading the recipe pages of my mum and dad's *Daily Mail* Weekend Magazine and sometimes my nan's copy of *Take a Break*.

Some mornings, I'd wake up and ask my mum if I'd been shouting out in my sleep because I was terrified I'd somehow unconsciously announced to my whole family that I was gay. I would be so exhausted trying to keep the lid on all these pressure cookers all the time, making sure no one knew anything about me while at the same time trying to blend in with lad and ladette culture – I was constantly tired and, at the same time, tired of everything around me.

I'd whine that I was bored. 'Well, what do you want to do?' my parents would shout-ask me and I would have absolutely no idea. I didn't know what options were available and I hadn't really had a chance to consider what I liked – the whole of school was basically a training in getting on with things you probably don't like.

I wanted to dress up in Victorian clothing and pretend I was in another era. I didn't tell them this though – I just did it. I'd always enjoyed wearing suits because they'd made me feel like a grown-up, someone who was in charge of his life. In addition to the waistcoats and handkerchiefs in my pocket, I now carried a briefcase to school and even a long umbrella, which I used as a walking cane. Sometimes I'd even wear a bow tie, which I'd taught myself to tie properly just to try to impress people.

'Oh . . . wow,' they'd say, unimpressed.

The classic Bromley response to this sort of behaviour would be, 'Look at him! Who does he think he is?!' This would be in their heads, of course, but I could almost hear them because they thought it so loudly. My parents were protective and also alarmed.

'You asked me what I wanted to do and this is what I want to do!'

If my parents' eyebrows could rise any further, they would have flown straight off the top of their heads. 'We didn't mean dress up like Charles Dickens – we meant doing something like ten-pin bowling in Bexleyheath or bouldering or joining the Boys Brigade!'

My other act of teenage rebellion was that I would spend my Saturdays travelling to London to go to the vintage-clothing shops and markets that existed in corners of the capital for the few people who, like me, loved pretending it was another era.

My grandmother was horrified at these expeditions to buy, as she saw it, remnants of the past (she could remember the poverty and the wars) and would slam down her toast (she always seemed to be eating toast) to say her catchphrase, 'I'm worried about you,' and would turn to my mum, 'I'm worried about that boy,' and then come back to me with, 'You frighten the life out of me!' Admittedly I probably did look like a ghost. If I tried to explain myself she'd say, 'All right, all right – well, I'll never come round here again,' and if I said anything back to that she'd say, 'Well, you'll be sorry when I'm gone.' It could be quite an emotional rollercoaster with Nan.

Mum would say nothing as she'd already made her feelings clear: it's disgusting to wear second-hand clothes because someone has probably died in them, they'll give you fleas and they'll bring in rats – don't bring them into the house. For this reason, anything I did buy would have to stay in the garage.

Dad, on the other hand, didn't get involved in these discussions. A coach driver at this point and a logistics man through and through, he would be much more interested in my travel arrangements and also my safety from muggers. His tip was to never put up a fight, but always look tough, like you might put up a fight so that a would-be mugger would think you'd be more trouble than you're worth.

Similarly, he'd tell me, 'Always look like you know where you're going, even if you don't know where you're going,' which can actually be quite exhausting. 'When you walk around do it with purpose and a stern face, as though you might have a fight with anyone (but don't). Keep the majority of your cash in your sock but always have a ten-pound note to hand in your pocket so if you do get mugged you can give them that quickly.' (Muggers always want to get away quickly, especially from me because I looked like a very purposeful, slightly aggressive Isambard Kingdom Brunel.)

My best purchases included a dinner jacket, which the tailor had pleasingly put the date in – 1937 – and a bowler hat, which didn't really fit my massive head but I could squeeze my cranium into it sometimes if I wasn't thinking too much that day.

What I really wanted was a silk top hat, but they are notoriously difficult to find because my head is so big and also the factory in France where the special silk plush was made closed in the 1960s. The two brothers who owned the factory apparently had a huge argument and smashed up the machinery, which to my mind only added to the romance of the situation. I thought if I could find a top hat that fitted, I could actually be Fred Astaire, though it had eluded me that I could not tap dance.

It was at this point that an old friend stepped into my life: Miss Hammond. When I was six years old, my mum had noticed that I had some eccentric tendencies and decided that I needed a dramatic outlet. So she took the tea cosy off my head and drove me to an audition for the local theatre school, which operated above a launderette next to a fish and chip shop on Belmont Parade.

The Patricia Hammond School of Dramatic Art required that I arrive on my own. I pushed the door to be greeted by a sign which said *NO FISH AND CHIPS – WAITING ROOM UPSTAIRS!* I remember being a little scared of this new world, but something intrigued me enough to carry on and not run back to the car where Mum was waiting.

I climbed the carpeted stairs and was immediately impressed by the framed pictures of stars who had appeared alongside pupils of the school in the local pantomime. Adorning the wood-cladded walls were photos of Parisian pierrots (these sad clowns in their ruffled collars a reminder of Miss Hammond's glamorous time in Paris) alongside Danny La Rue and Nicholas

Parsons, Roy Hudd and even Bonnie Langford. All I knew was that it was showbiz, and I wanted to be part of it.

In preparation for my audition I had rehearsed a poem – 'I'm Busy Busy Busy Said the Bee' – which I performed, I'm sure, very movingly to the school's principal, Patricia Hammond herself. I am not sure how strict these auditions were, but I wonder now if they weren't wisely designed to make sure Miss Hammond would not have to deal with too many insufferable brats on a regular basis. Despite the fact that I am sure I was very precocious, I still passed muster and was allowed to attend classes every Saturday afternoon.

Miss Hammond was a very dignified person and very different from the other adults I knew, who were mainly dinner ladies. She had a soft blow-wave perm and very exotic perfume and spoke quietly in a way that commanded attention. Not like the dinner ladies who seemed to always be bellowing, 'Errrrrrrr!' across playgrounds and pointing at children while they tried to remember their names.

The Saturday classes involved sitting in a circle alongside other precocious children and each in turn performing a poem on which Miss Hammond would then give feedback and which we would be expected to practise before the next lesson the following week. Occasionally a glass of water would be brought in for her by her devoted husband, John – a quiet man with a very kind smile.

Though I had kept in contact with Miss Hammond (out of respect I would never call her by her first name, Patricia), it wasn't until I received a card from her as a teenager that our friendship really bloomed. The card explained in a manner that was effortlessly dignified that after an illness, her beloved husband John had died and she was heartbroken.

It was time for my first condolence letter using that letter-writing kit I had bought in WHSmith's with the vouchers I had been given for my birthday. A condolence letter is perhaps the most formal of all communications and the Victorians, even Queen Victoria herself, revelled in the rituals of mourning.

I wrote a very long letter about how sorry I was to hear this and how I imagined she must be feeling. Having never written a condolence letter before, I showed it to my dad who glanced at it briefly and then said, 'No, no, no, you don't need to write all that! You just put: "Thoughts and prayers, Tom". That's all you need. That'll be lovely. She won't want to read much more than that, honestly, Tom.'

So that's what I wrote. It wasn't that my dad was being unkind when he said this, he's from an era when it was considered undignified, selfish even, to say too much because you'd end up saying more about yourself and this was supposed to be a moment for someone else.

Despite what I worried was quite a curt message, I received a phone call inviting me to afternoon tea with Miss Hammond in her conservatory. To me, at this point in my life, this was everything. Finally someone understood that I was the sort of sixteen-year-old who liked being invited round to tea. In a conservatory. Not running round with a J-Cloth while school friends went to town on each other on the kitchen worktop.

'Oh, yes, I'd be delighted!' I said, in an even posher voice than my normal one.

'Bit over the top with the accent there, eh, Tom?' said Dad, who'd been passing by the phone.

I didn't care – this was finally my chance to be me. I knew exactly what to wear – my bow tie with my dinner jacket from 1937, even though it was afternoon tea and not dinner.

Dad drove me there despite Miss Hammond living approximately fifteen minutes' walk away, and I had literally nothing else to do, but, as ever, my dad loved to give lifts. Mum also gave me a punnet of strawberries to take round.

Walking through the simple front door of Miss Hammond's house, I realised it was everything I dreamed a house could be – it was full of the smell of incense, a Grecian statue holding a torch stood proudly next to the phone table, a pink marble fireplace with an enormous Japanese fan above it graced the sitting room. The windows were adorned with taffeta curtains blocking the ugly outside world, while an actual chaise longue stood in the bay window. The dining room had murals of ancient Rome and a thick red curtain covering up the tumble dryer.

I sat very upright on the wicker chair in the conservatory, underneath the grape vine that draped around the edges of the glass room. '. . . Well, Tom, we all have to remember, it's so important to be ourselves in this world. None of us are here for a long time.'

'Yes, indeed – people find that so difficult to remember, don't they?' I was someone who said 'indeed' now, without my classmates there to laugh at me. I was so proud of myself for being the person I always dreamed I could be – in a conservatory too, as if I were in *The Importance of Being Earnest*. I was so delighted with myself, I totally missed that I'd been given an open door to finally come out to somebody.

'Yes, they do – but you're a much more sensitive soul than most and that's a wonderful thing. As I always say about my house, it's a place for outsiders and individuals with character – you are always welcome here. I've been working in the theatre a long time – perhaps I know you better than you know yourself?'

Not wanting to say anything too verbose in case I was 'over-doing it' as Dad would say, I nodded my head solemnly and thanked her. I had literally no idea that she was trying to help me. Before I knew it, it was time for Dad to pick me up and I took my bowler hat and said goodbye.

'And, Sir Tom' – (she had given me a title by this point – this had truly been a great afternoon) – 'would you like to come and see a production of Gilbert and Sullivan's *HMS Pinafore* with me next week in a garden in Croydon?'

The gay gods were smiling down on me from the walls of the dining room that afternoon – of course, I was delighted to accept!

The evening arrived. I wore my white trousers (which used to be my dad's when he played cricket that one time), my blazer with the brassy buttons and to complete the look, a straw boater hat. I thought I looked like a young aristocrat going to a regatta, but, in truth, I probably looked to the outside world exactly like every other closeted gay sixteen-year-old out with his recently widowed childhood drama teacher at a light operetta in a Croydon garden.

If the people in my year could see me now, how drab their gelled hair and 'getting off with people from the school down the road' would seem. We watched theatre in people's gardens and ate cucumber sandwiches from a Tupperware that Miss Hammond had brought. Afterwards we ran into an old friend of Miss Hammond. 'Sir Tom, you must meet Lady Beryl.' I wondered if everyone had such exotic made-up titles in this new world. It was like the back pages of *Hello!* magazine.

I don't know how many aristocrats are called Beryl, but she seemed nice enough, if lacking in fun. I got the sense that she could tolerate eccentricity, but not too much. She'd enjoy a musical, but she wouldn't buy the soundtrack. She seemed a bit bemused by me: a sixteen-year-old dressed like he should be selling ice creams, accompanying his grieving teacher friend.

Miss Hammond announced, 'Lady Beryl is coming to lunch next Saturday and—'

And I leapt in with 'I'd love to!'

I'll never know if I was actually being invited or not, but it didn't matter, I was just having a wonderful time. Beryl looked horrified, but this was nothing new.

'In fact,' I said, getting overexcited, 'rather than being a guest, why don't I be your butler?'

Miss Hammond looked delighted. '*Yes!* That would be marvellous! Wouldn't that be a scream? Beryl, isn't he the most wonderful young person? Such an eccentric, I love it! Well, we all are, aren't we? Thank God, we're not all normal.'

'Yes,' said Beryl, lying.

I was able to deal with Beryl's general dismissiveness towards me because at school I was starting to feel more confident amongst my peer group. I was almost annoyed that the weirder I became, the less they seemed to mind. If anything, wearing a bow tie, carrying an umbrella and a briefcase and slicking my hair back like Noël Coward seemed to make people want to say hello more.

What's more, role models were starting to appear on television in dramas and even in soaps. *EastEnders* had their first gay couple, *Brookside* had a lesbian kiss and *Queer as Folk* had finally aired on Channel 4. I'd watched it on the old black-and-white TV in my room I'd been given by one of the neighbours. To stop my parents from hearing, I'd watched it with the sound turned right down which, combined with the black-and-white picture, made it seem like a Manchester-themed Charlie Chaplin porn film (minus the piano accompaniment).

If I'm honest, I probably could have come out to my friends at school at this point without it being much of an issue, and I doubt any of them would have been that surprised. The problem was less them and more me. I absolutely didn't want to, and I hated these untidy feelings I couldn't control and the tearaway fantasies about any boy I came into contact with. This surely wasn't how a nice young man should be feeling. If I am being totally honest, I categorically and absolutely loathed myself.

All the grades I achieved and the attempts at being a model student should have been leading to a moment when I didn't dislike myself any more, but the moment never came. I kept working towards something else, assuming at the next hurdle the clouds would lift – winning the school piano competition, joining the debating team – but nothing seemed to make a difference.

It's for this reason I think a lot of adults love business class on airplanes: 'I can afford to travel in a big chair, so maybe I'm OK now?'

The self-loathing had crept in somewhere early on and wouldn't be shaken off with any amount of well-meant head tilts and hands on my shoulder whenever I tried to tell people how I felt – now it just seemed to be part of me. With no way to get rid of it, my best option was to continue to distract myself with my Victorian fantasy life.

The day of being a butler for Miss Hammond arrived and I put on a tailcoat, which I'd bought the previous weekend. Walking downstairs, I dreaded what I'd have to hear from

Mum and Dad. Perhaps what was much more disappointing was that they didn't say anything; by this point they were either resigned to my eccentric antics or using a different tactic to dissuade me from continuing on this path.

'Oh, you look nice,' said Mum. 'Going to give us a tap dance, are you?'

'Obviously not,' I mumbled in an irritated teenage voice.

'Do you want a lift?' said Dad.

When we arrived at Miss Hammond's, I waited for Dad to drive off before I rang the bell because a butler would hardly get their dad to drop them off. This certainly didn't happen in *The Remains of the Day*. Remains of the Gay, perhaps.

'Sir Tom!' said Miss Hammond, her arms held aloft to greet me. 'Come in! Let the buttling commence!'

We had an hour to get the table set. I knew exactly what to do with the cutlery after my dinner party efforts the previous summer, and napkin folding was something I could do with my eyes closed. In fact, given half a chance, I probably would have done it with my eyes closed just to show off how special I thought I was.

It was decided that lunch for Beryl would be served in the garden. Miss Hammond had even got out her pastel-coloured iridescent wine glasses. The salmon main course was poaching in the oven. Everything was ready when Beryl rang the bell.

Miss Hammond went to answer the door and then stopped. 'Oh no! This is your job, of course!'

'Ah, yes, of course,' I trilled, both of us beside ourselves with excitement.

'Good afternoon, Lady Beryl. Miss Hammond is expecting you in the garden.'

Beryl looked horrified again. 'Yes.'

Maybe she just had a miserable-looking face. Maybe she was embarrassed at finding herself in the middle of this immersive theatre piece against her will, annoyed that her catch-up with her friend 'Pat' was going to be interrupted by me. Again.

'Please follow me,' I said, doing my best *Upstairs Downstairs* impersonation, but Beryl was having none of it and pushed straight past. Despite my attempts to pretend we were in Buckingham Palace, miserable Beryl could see the kitchen door to the garden was already open.

'Drinks are served – would madam care for a glass of wine?'

'Yes,' said Beryl, miserably.

I left them to talk in the garden, secretly smiling inside because I had finally found my purpose. I knew what I would be – a butler! It was perfect. I could wear old-fashioned clothing and take pride in starching my collars and always looking immaculate. Finally, my obsession with old-fashioned etiquette and napkins would be embraced and even celebrated.

Better than all of this, I wouldn't have to worry about my own feelings getting hurt by straight boys who'd never love me back or trying to fit in with drunk parties in a kitchen because my life would be dedicated to facilitating someone else's life. Of course, no one would question my lack of a partner because I would be too busy ironing a newspaper and pouring drinks. It really was the perfect plan.

I took the salmon from the oven and arranged it on the serving platter with lemon wedges and the hollandaise sauce in the sauce boat on the edge of the platter as planned. It looked to my eccentric teenage eye, utterly marvellous. I had heated the serving plate by placing it in the oven because that's what my mum and dad always did. Picking up the salmon, it had not occurred to me just how hot the plate had become and while walking it to the table and trying to maintain a stately pace, it was increasingly apparent to me that I was burning my hand.

I sped up my pace and ended up crashing the dish onto the table in such a hurry that Beryl's horrified face was now tinged with genuine fear. I managed to slam it on the edge of the table with a loud, 'Owwww!' and because it was on the edge of the table, the plate upended, tipping most of the contents onto Beryl's dress. She grabbed the platter to steady it back onto the table and in doing so also burnt her hand. 'Owwwwww!' she screamed too.

Standing up and shaking her burnt hand, her dress now covered in lemon slices and hollandaise sauce, Miserable Beryl looked like she'd been at some sort of terrible al fresco paint-balling party.

Miss Hammond stood now too, imploring, 'Beryl, are you burnt?! I'll get some ice. Or an ambulance!'

'Yes' said Beryl, glaring at me as if to say, 'You fool.'

'Fetch some ice!' I was instructed. Even though I didn't know where the ice was, I was thrilled to be spoken to in such harsh terms like a real butler. I brought the ice. Miss Hammond took charge and pressed the ice cubes into Beryl's burnt hand. 'Is that any better?'

'I'm so sorry!' I said, flapping.

'Yes,' said Beryl, holding her chin up but also perhaps on the cusp of tears. Miss Hammond couldn't help glancing at her dress, a wry smile at just how awful it looked.

Beryl stayed for coffee and biscuits, but the mood had gone, Miss Hammond and I sadly aware of our folly in trying to create an imaginary world for the afternoon for Beryl to be a part of. I loomed in the background as goodbyes were said. 'I'll phone you in the week!' called Miss Hammond cheerily to Beryl as she clambered into her minicab.

'Yes,' said Beryl, waving with her burnt hand miserably.

Later, we sat in the garden as the stars began to come out. I'd done enough buttling for one day. I didn't think it was right to mention that Beryl clearly didn't like me. Apart from it seeming impolite, it was obvious.

'The world is just full of so many interesting people,' said Miss H. 'Isn't that a wonderful thing? And there's room for all of them!'

'Yes, I suppose that's true!' I didn't have much experience of interesting people, but I wasn't sure how Beryl could rank as one of them.

'What's your favourite film?' asked Miss Hammond.

Suddenly panicked, I was unable to choose between my back catalogue of critically acclaimed masterpieces, so quickly went for the first film that sprung to mind:

'*Independence Day.*' I instantly felt stupid for saying it – of all the films Miss Hammond would expect her butler friend to like, the one about aliens coming to take over the world was the last one I should have suggested. I'd been doing so well. effortlessly using words like 'indeed' in casual conversation. '. . . It's about aliens.'

'Well, that's the thing, isn't it? We all like different things, don't we? I love that.'

'Do you believe in aliens?' I asked. 'I just really think it would be so interesting if they existed.'

'Oh yes, definitely,' she said, pausing, and then gesturing around her. 'There has to be more to life than this.' We both sat in silence for a moment, listening to the traffic roar in the distance.

Two people, a generation apart, one denying his life had really begun, the other coming to terms with her loss; both brought together, trying to escape the here and now, for one moment, sat staring up at the night sky.

5

Working

'Rum baba, strawberry bavarois, lemon mousse? Or there's a sherry trifle on the second layer there, and an apple crumble as the hot option. I can also offer cheese and biscuits if sir was in the mood for something savoury?'

My first job was wheeling a dessert trolley around a golf-club dining room. It was still 1999 and I was still sixteen and closeted but with a penchant for showing off, which was in a bid to desperately hide that I was gay. I hadn't really experienced the outside world beyond school though I had now completed my GCSEs, including food technology in which I had got an A* (I knew all the correct fridge temperatures for ham) it turned out that my new skills were not universally appreciated.

'You've got to stop taking forever talking to people about fruit salad – we ain't got time! There's a hundred people out there, so if you turn that sweet trolley into a song and dance for every table, we'll be here all fucking day!' said one of my new colleagues. This first foray into the world of service was also starting to suggest that my dream of becoming a butler might not be quite as fulfilling as I'd hoped – I only liked the idea of formality when it was on my terms.

While the golf club was at times an odd place to work, with rigorous rules and occasional snobbery on one side and a salt-of-the-earth South London feel on the other, my colleagues did seem to care about me and wanted to include me, even though sometimes it was in quite unusual ways. For example, on one occasion, they took me to see my first football game, at Millwall. They paid for my ticket, drove me there and gave me a Millwall shirt to wear and gave me the advice 'Don't open your fucking mouth!' which, in retrospect, was probably meant with more kindness than I knew. Especially when, after the interval, I stood up to cheer when they scored a goal, not realising the teams had swapped ends.

I knew that I was getting ready for the next chapter in my life but I had no idea what that would involve, still reliant on whatever was offered to me by school. In the meantime, I was determined to master my new multistorey cake stand on wheels. The dessert trolley itself was made of three chipped melamine levels held together by wire, which curved up at the sides to stop a trifle wobbling into someone's lap. The wheels themselves were too small for the dense shag-pile carpet and would often get stuck taking corners, requiring either a three-point turn or for a member of the team to angrily come and help me lift it into position.

At the end of their meal, when people were busily enjoying one another's company, I would appear at their elbow and surprise the – often elderly – diners with my trilled announcement. 'Can I interest any of you in dessert?'

Without waiting for them to respond, I'd immediately embark on my ambitious whirlwind tour of the sweet options, embellished with my opinions and stories about how 'a fruit salad once broke my heart' and 'nothing says Sunday like a strawberry flan', even referring to the sweet trolley itself as 'my cabriolet of puddings'. It was nonsense, but I felt alive. People loved it – or at least I thought they did.

I thought their eyes were lighting up but in retrospect maybe they were just opening wider to signal to their fellow diners, *We need to get out of here – make him stop.* To my mind, I just loved pleasing people and surprising them with how much I cared about their dessert experience. I longed for their approval, even more so if they looked like the sort of stern conservative group who might not like me – these were my favourite challenge.

Frequently, I'd get to the end of my rhapsody and be met with, 'Sorry, I was a million miles away could you run through that again?' I'd try to suppress a disdainful glare as I went back to the beginning and began the performance again. Even then they needed to be reminded of the second or third option on my cavalcade of tarts, flans and desserts. 'Oh, you know what, actually I'm full,' they'd concede, and I would be furious, barely hiding my withering stare as I walked behind one end of the trolley to jump start it onto the next table.

Back then, the dining room where I performed my flan-based monologues was typical of any traditional golf club around the turn of the millennium. It was covered in huge glass cabinets displaying golf trophies, awards and antique golf clubs. Having no interest in the sport itself, I felt bored just looking at it. Above the carvery was perhaps the only splash of glamour – a portrait of the Queen wearing the Sovereign of the Garter cloak draped over one shoulder as she gazed regally, almost coquettishly, down at us and the napkins stuffed into wine glasses and the legions of blazer-wearing men (wearing a jacket was compulsory in the dining room).

As with every golf club, there were sweeping fairways and immaculate putting greens but in a cruel design flaw of the club-house, the dining room had been built with no view of the course itself and instead occupied a gloomy position at the back overlooking the car park and the bins. It was as if making the experience of dining too enjoyable would be an embarrassment – an affectation – that would put people off their meals.

The corridors of the clubhouse were lined with photo-graphic portraits of past club captains, all sat sternly in blazers to represent the dignity of the club. The ladies' captains had a separate corridor of portraits, which I preferred because it included my favourite – a captain from the early 1980s with a tight perm, pussy-bow blouse and massive square glasses with darkened lenses. She looked like Dustin Hoffman in *Tootsie* or Jane Fonda in *9 to 5*.

When I wasn't dragging a trifle around the Sunday-lunch customers, I was required to polish cutlery by dipping it in a combination of hot water and vinegar and rubbing it with a tea towel. It was something the whole team had to do, usually near the end of service. On my first shift, I picked up a towel from the work bench to begin this new and exciting task alongside everyone else. One member of the team, who had bobbed hair like a mum in her forties even though she was only in her twenties, seemed to be angry about something, but I didn't know what.

'Oi! Where's my towel?' she snapped at me. 'Did you take my towel?' I went red – I didn't realise that people had their own tea towels! It was my first day in the world of work and I was still grasping the rules. 'Give it back to me!' she said, snatching it out of my hand like I'd tried to steal her child. 'Get your own fucking tea towel!'

At the end of this first shift, Dad picked me up – because he loves giving lifts – and I told him I never wanted to go back there again.

'You're too sensitive!' I didn't think I was too sensitive – I thought I was just the right amount of sensitive. In fairness to Dad, I think he felt that if I was going to carry on living in the world with eccentric tendencies, I should probably learn to toughen up as soon as possible.

'. . . At least I'll be getting some money to spend.'

'I wouldn't spend it – you want to save that money. You never know when you might need it for going to university or something else worthwhile.'

Since my earnings were in the bank and there was nothing to splash out on, I lived for pushing that dessert trolley. The rest of the time when I had to do mundane tasks like polishing cutlery, I'd disappear into daydreams about what I wanted to do with my life, which at this time mainly involved being friends with Elton John and wearing tailored suits every day.

As well as taking too long to perform the trolley description, I also got in trouble for taking too much time presenting everything as the plates were too small and each presentation ended up looking overcrowded. The pavlova looked like it was bursting off the edges of its plate – like my performance, it was just a bit too big for this small suburban golf-club dining room.

On one occasion, I realised why my colleagues needed me to hurry up. I was enjoying taking my time singing the praises of a French apple flan when I heard, '*You wanna what?!*'

A female diner shouted behind me at another woman across the gangway.

'*What are you saying?!*' the other woman responded aggressively.

'I just said we've been waiting for ages for it to come round and I don't like being ignored! I don't want to be sat here—'

Now both standing, towering over the other diners sat in their golf blazers: 'You wanna calm down – you can see he's only doing his best!'

The other diners, in typical Bromley fashion, tried to ignore the shouting.

'*You* wanna shut your face!' The other diners gasped and reached for their paper napkins as though they might have to use them in self-defence, presumably some sort of martial-arts-themed Morris dance.

Then, in a flash, one woman stomped across the gangway to the other and engaged in what can only be described as punchy, slappy, face-pushing fighting in the middle of the dining room. All because I'd taken so long to get to them with my flan and sponge trolley. I was horrified, but mainly thrilled. A member of the team flew across the room and stood between them, even though she barely came up to the two fighting women's chests. '*Calm down! Sit down . . . Siiiiiiitt doooouwn.*' She handled it all with ease, like a prison warden, which maybe she had been at some stage.

Both tables felt it was time to leave, encouraged strongly by the disdainful stares and napkin waving from around the room. I imagined they carried on their shouting and shoving in the car park. *I* certainly hoped so.

The prison-warden-cum-waitress came over to me next. 'Do you *see* now why I tell you to hurry up with the fucking thing?! These people aren't patient!'

It wasn't a 'fucking thing'. It was my project – my fancy way of interacting with diners while always being on the move. Since I was too scared to learn to drive, this was my equivalent to owning my first car.

I just felt things could be done better – with more elan, more elegance, and if everyone was given enough time, they could make things truly beautiful so that everything in the world could be exquisite. Imagine a world filled with perfect beauty, where everyone was able to do their very best for one another – what a wonderful world that would be.

My mum's advice for when I was frustrated with the world of work was to use my imagination. She was now working as a receptionist for a firm in Orpington. Reception staff are often seen as the lowest rung in the secretarial ladder (secretarial staff are often very snooty about their positions) but my mum didn't care, and as the first point of contact for visitors to the firm, she would pride herself on looking immaculate, buying flowers with her own money for the front desk and greeting everyone with a smile.

When people at the company would speak to her abruptly or fuss around the petty politics that affect all small organisations (who gets to wear a high-vis vest during a fire drill, who puts up the Christmas tree), Mum used to tell me she'd make it more bearable by imagining they were just characters in a story.

Seeing the cold and unemotional head of finance or the bumptious company secretary dressed up in a top hat or a bonnet like people in a Dickens novel made them much easier to bear. Suddenly the world was just a big story book populated by all these characters with their silly neuroses and particularities – they seemed so silly. It was all just a huge television adaptation of a classic novel in which I just happened to be the narrator. It certainly helped me and I started using the time polishing cutlery to imagine myself as Little Nell.

I got the job there because my dad was a member of the golf club. He had joined when I was about eight and we were all very proud of his membership with the great and the good of Bromley. I thought it was the most glamorous place I had ever been to because crisps and scampi fries were served in small metal dishes with their own pedestals and white wine was on tap – literally, it came out of a tap – and was served to my mum in a small fluted glass.

The golf club had rules and regulations banning any kind of denim, insisting that shorts be knee length and worn with high socks and formal white shoes (never trainers). Blazers had to be worn with a tie on Sundays. I am happy to say that since then, the golf club, at which my dad is still involved, is a much more progressive and friendly place free of the snobberies of yester-year. The people my dad would refer to as 'the old gits' have gone to the clubhouse in the sky, and now it's a much younger and friendlier crowd.

Back then, I found out about the dress code the hard way when I was taken to the golf club for my birthday, wearing my new jeans from Marks and Spencer, and was given money to go and buy myself a Coke at the bar. Sprightly faced, I paid for my drink and then was told by the surly bar staff aggressively drying a glass, 'You can't wear jeans in here – it's against the rules.'

'Oh, is it?'

'I should throw you out.'

'I'm sorry – it's my birthday today.'

This seemed to piss her off even more. 'You can't wear jeans at the golf club. Doesn't matter what "day" it is.' Here was the classic Bromley shh-ing – a sense that you should never get too happy or confident or someone would tear you down.

All those years ago, golf clubs were very old-fashioned and not just in their outfits. There was an area at the club that made my mum furious: the men's bar – a separate bar reserved exclusively for male members (of the club), filled with smoke (when people could still smoke indoors) and the din of a television blaring out sports over the men's grumbling.

In protest, when Mum had to go to a dinner dance there, she would deviate there from a trip to the ladies' loos to sit on the faded green armchairs, wiggling in each one, mocking what was so special about this sacred space before one of the staff would raise an eyebrow and look like they were about to tell her off and she'd hurriedly leave. Happily, this relic was abandoned years ago and I like to think it was in no small part due to Mum's sit-in protests.

My brother liked the club because he was naturally good at golf. I, on the other hand, liked the idea of golf mainly for the outfits – the plus fours and tartan flat caps and brogue shoes. When Dad tried to teach me when I was aged seven, I could barely even hit the ball. If I did manage to, it just skidded a few feet in front of me and then landed in a bush while my brother seemed to send it sweeping gracefully into the air every time, even though he was four years younger than me.

This resulted in me throwing a tantrum and, in my blind fury, I kicked my dad's golf bag, threw the golf club itself (it actually went much further than the ball had gone so maybe I could have been a javelin thrower) as I tried to expel an uncontrollable rage that ran all down my leg – like an itch in my shin bone which I could only scratch by stamping. Dad was calm about it (members of the golf club were expected to behave with decorum at all times), but without ever speaking it was decided that I would never play golf again.

All those years later, if I was to have any involvement in the club, it would only be in the catering department.

I worked there every weekend throughout the sixth form, and I grew to feel more confident about my dessert-trolley wheeling. Some people said they came for the lunch and stayed for the trifles, which I took as a personal compliment. However, there were still moments I didn't enjoy, and the task I hated most was 'bottling up', which involved restocking the fridges with the small bottles of mixers. It was fiddly and took a long time because I'd have to move the old bottles to the front and make sure the new ones were wiped down because, as was explained to me, 'dogs might've pissed on them when they were in the crate'. It really was a glamorous world I was operating in, though not one without its opinions.

One evening, I was entrusted with the bottling-up task while at the other end of the long bar sat one of the opinionated old guard, an 'old git', on the faded green velvet barstools in front of the cigarette machine. I could hear them chatting casually. 'I mean, I don't mind them, don't mind them at all really,' I overheard coming from their end of the bar, 'some of them are very nice people.'

I wondered what they were talking about as I wiped off another bottle of Schweppes tonic water. 'I mean, look at him, he's one – he's a very nice fella, I suppose,' I had to assume they meant me since he'd just pointed directly at me. 'So, I guess some of them are nice.'

'Yes, I suppose so,' said his wife absently.

My blood ran cold – if they were talking about what I thought they were, I was perplexed at how they could know. I hadn't told them anything about me, in fact, I was exhausted from hiding everything. Was it the way I wiped dog piss off the bottles? Or maybe the way I bent over from the waist to pick them up out of the crate? Surely it wasn't the way I skipped around with the dessert trolley?

They hadn't said anything negative per se. I felt a sense of shame at being exposed. And besides, it wasn't their thing to talk about. I was humiliated at being judged while in my confusion there was also indignation – 'Who did they think they were? People aren't here to be judged like that, behind their back, still in ear shot'.

A more confident person might have complained, but I wasn't sure if there was anything to complain about, really. I could hardly have talked to someone about it. 'Mum, they said I was gay!' 'Well, are you?' 'Yes – but no!' This was exactly the sort of conversation I was working so hard to avoid.

In any case, at the time, it was in a sense, illegal for me to be gay. The age of consent for same-sex couples was eighteen, two years older than for straight people. Earlier in the year, a gay pub in Soho had been nail-bombed. There was no legal protection for discrimination against gay people. We were banned from serving in the military (which was actually fine by me), we couldn't get married or even have a civil partnership and Section 28 was still in force, meaning schools couldn't say to kids that it was OK to be gay. I didn't know anything about politics at this time; I wasn't getting some sort of gay newsletter, social media hadn't been invented and people didn't talk openly about this sort of thing, but these rules set a tone in the world, without me realising it, and actions spoke loud in the absence of positive words.

When the nail bomb went off in the Admiral Duncan pub on Old Compton Street on 30 April 1999, there was a heaviness at our kitchen table as we watched the news. There was shock at something so horrific – the scenes of young men stumbling out of a pub covered in blood – but at the same time, there was silence. Looking back, I realise without us having ever discussed it, it was a confirmation of my parents' biggest fear – was this the sort of violence their son might be letting himself in for?

There were no tools or guidance for them to discuss any of it, and, as a result, I was left wondering if they even knew I was gay. Yes, there were the Noël Coward songs and elaborate dinner parties for teachers and dressing up as Julie Walters and a propensity to talk endlessly with classmates' mothers about hysterectomies – but was this proof enough? It was impossible to know.

But if what they saw on the news that night was the least they could expect for me, it's little wonder they didn't want to talk about it.

However, things couldn't exist like this forever, and suddenly, one day, I was offered a lifeline – the possibility of a life away from these petty tea–towel disputes. An escape which combined all of my favourite things: snobbery, National Trust–style buildings and a sense of history.

I went to Cambridge University.

For the day.

I loved studying history at A-Level, the politics and the complexity of generations of people thinking and living; how it manifests in unusual and unexpected uprisings, even though, with hindsight, everything seems so predictable. The pursuit of understanding our shared past feels like the most important thing in understanding our present day.

In our increasingly tabloid-information age, it feels like the process of studying history is more relevant than ever. As well as teaching us to acknowledge what has come before, it gives us perspective and context. It trains us to take a step back from our emotional response to acknowledge nuance and detail, and it helps us work out if the source of information is genuine – are we being manipulated by an historian, journalist or politician? It is the opposite of the 280 characters of a tweet or the impulse to have a fight over a dessert trolley.

We all have biases, of course – a totally objective telling of past events is an impossibility, but that doesn't mean we shouldn't strive for it. Some people might even suggest that my telling of the events in this very book might be biased, based solely on my desire to always seem witty and important, and that your understanding of it all is distorted by me. But, of course, those people are idiots and should be disregarded. You need only believe everything I say.

The misery of the past and the suffering and oppression of generations of powerless people is so important to understand if we are ever to value how far we have come and how far we have yet to go. I also still really liked the clothes.

Our history classroom was a draughty and gloomy room upstairs in the Victorian buildings that housed the sixth form at our school. There was nothing on the walls, the white paint peeling off and occasionally patched-up with mismatched colours, which always seemed to be light blue. We'd usually have to spend the first five minutes getting the classroom ready to study in as chairs had been thrown on the floor, the seat broken off from its legs, and the desks had their tops stripped back to the MDF underneath. Lots of young people in the school didn't like being there, and without means to express themselves, they took it out on the furniture.

Our history teacher Miss Wickens got us to chat about things in such a broad way. I'd never had someone open my mind and make me feel so enthusiastic. Because of her, I loved reading history textbooks; the essays she set weren't chores to be completed but a means of discussing and refining what I was thinking about anyway.

It was Miss Wickens who presented the astonishing notion that I could apply for Cambridge. This was a bombshell, a revelation – I didn't understand how these things worked, nor whether I'd be qualified to even send in an application form.

It became my absolute focus – Mum and Dad loved the idea, the neighbours were already impressed and, moreover, no one in our family had ever been to university. The buildings had all the old-fashioned grandeur about them that Mum and I loved on our trips to National Trust properties. In a way, it would be like I was finally travelling back in time.

I could be like the characters in *Brideshead Revisited*. All those formal dinners, the napkins and choirs singing by candlelight like I'd seen on the BBC on Christmas Eve.

Sadly, Miss Wickens left before I started my application. I had no insight but had to choose one of the many colleges within the university to apply to. Choosing a college seemed to make it all the more unnecessarily complicated. I settled on one called Clare College because it had nice windows and 'Clare' was the name of my form tutor and I liked her. I was also told it wasn't too grand for me – the famous Kings College was very political and they wouldn't be interested in me whereas places like Trinity College were only interested in kids from boarding schools. I gleaned this from a nice teacher who had gone to Anglia Ruskin University up the road.

Now seventeen and at the start of my last year at school, I sent in the application and I was invited for an interview. It's been said before by other people, much more eloquent than I, that the buildings seem to have been designed to intimidate people who aren't used to such grandeur. However, with me this wasn't the case as I wasn't intimidated at all. If anything I loved it too much. I'd been educated at a suburban comprehensive with cucumber slices stuck to the wall, but these ancient quadrangles and Palladian pillars were exactly the sort of architecture I'd always dreamed I belonged in.

Mum and Dad drove me there – for Dad, the *ultimate* lift – and they insisted on making a day of it. In fact, they were so excited they booked to go to a carol concert, of course by candlelight, and a tea room for scones.

At the allotted time, I waved them off at the ornate gate at the front of the college, where a porter in a bowler hat was there to escort me to the designated room. I had to restrain myself from getting too excited at a man wearing a bowler hat for his job and not just for fun. I wasn't intimidated by the buildings but, looking back, I realise now that focusing on all these things meant I was perhaps in the wrong mindset.

I had to wait on a cold stairwell in a tower before being invited into a small study by two history professors to sit on a chair facing both of them, like a police interview in a television drama. The two men didn't seem quite as I expected – both in their fifties, they wore jumpers and open-necked shirts and not tweed blazers under academic gowns as I'd imagined from watching *Inspector Morse*. They were bespectacled to fit the stereotype and were nice and polite and cheerful – in a way that people are nice and polite and cheerful if they've never been told to 'get their own fucking tea towel.'

They asked me a series of questions about history, but foolishly I just kept telling them that I loved the building and I loved Noël Coward and if I came to university there, I would throw myself into the extracurricular drama stuff and I'd really enjoy the community of it all, and did I mention that I loved the buildings? It was like I was on a game show telling the host that despite not winning, I'd 'had a lovely day'.

I made sure I shook their hands while making eye contact and said thank you for meeting me, and then I left. I met Mum and Dad and told them it went well, not quite ready to accept that maybe it hadn't.

A month later, a couple of days after Christmas, a letter arrived and Dad ran up the stairs in his dressing gown (funny place to have some stairs) to wake me up and say a letter had arrived! It was a normal envelope with a one-page letter inside, which I knew wasn't a good sign as it meant there was not much to convey. 'Due to the exceptionally high standard this year amongst applicants blah blah blah.' It was a no-thanks. Dad looked crushed, but he tried to keep a smile on his face to stop me from feeling bad.

The college gave feedback, something about, 'We very much enjoyed meeting Thomas and while he is clearly a very enthusiastic student, we felt he had a tendency to jump in with an answer rather than consider a more thoughtful response.'

Looking back, I realise that, of course, I jumped in fast – I had been taught to be the most polite boy in the whole wide world and if an adult asks you a question, you should respond to it quickly and positively. My whole life had been about trying to seem polite and nice, charming even, to make people like me (and the desserts on my trolley). I didn't know you were supposed to leave them sat there while you pondered something insightful to say. What if during that pause they realised that I was gay?

Of course for students with insight into the Oxford and Cambridge system (largely through parental experience of the Oxford and Cambridge system or private schooling where more of the teachers seemed to have gone there) they knew which college to apply to and how to behave in the interview. They also knew not to apply to the pretty colleges because they were already oversubscribed with idiots like me trying to live in a period drama. Instead of applying for popular subjects like history, they knew to apply for obscure ones like Anglo-Saxon Norse and Celtic at one of the brutalist grey colleges round the corner and then just change subject when they got there. I think it's insider knowledge like this that cements class so rigidly.

Sadly, after all this, history had lost its lustre. In the A-Level course we no longer got to do the big dramatic stuff and were spending ages on analysing farming equipment and the importance of the spinning jenny in the Industrial Revolution.

I was becoming more and more despondent as I felt truly stuck; I had a job I wasn't very good at and I'd worked flat out at history A-Level to be told I 'jumped in too fast' – what was all this work for? I longed for a means of escape. My uniform for the golf club was a white shirt with a black bow tie. I made sure I tied my own bow tie and I had taken to slicking my hair back with Brylcreem like a waiter on the *Titanic*.

'Can't you wear it like the other boys do? It just looks like it's scraped back like a vampire,' my mum would say, correctly. This was ten years before vintage clothing was deemed cool. If anything, I like to think I created the whole look, though there is no proof of this and it is very unlikely since I rarely left Bromley.

The golf club had taught me I was tough enough to deal with at least some of the outside world, but the outside world was getting louder and louder.

Barely a year later, while my friends prepared to go to their university places, I had given up on the idea of further education, and I was back working behind the bar and as a new project I'd decided to see if I could grow a beard in a bid to feel more grown-up.

A woman rushed into the mens' bar – the men all gasped, scandalised – she shouted, 'Put on the telly! Put on the BBC – my dad's just rung up to say put on the BBC!'

We changed the channel from the tedious sport with its laconic score boards and soporific commentators to see a high-rise building on fire. Somewhere in New York. Something about a plane and then as we stopped drying the glasses from the glass washer, another plane flew into the World Trade Centre.

'You shouldn't have a beard in a kitchen, it's unhygienic,' said my colleague, oblivious to the images on the TV.

Staring past him at the screen, I said, 'But this isn't a kitchen, it's a bar.' I really wanted to scream, '*You're not my boss! And look at what's happening in the world!*'

'Doesn't matter – you can't grow a beard, it's against hygiene regulations.' He was trying to make me feel like I did when I was a child, wearing jeans on my birthday against the golf-club rules, but I was sick of rules by this point. Besides, rules didn't matter any more – the world was about to change dramatically.

There was suddenly a still silence and a clarity in my mind. And then I realised it was because the television channel had been changed, and it wasn't showing the billowing smoke of

New York any more, but the golf scores again. I marched up to the grumpy-looking old–git golfer sat next to it. 'What happened to the television?' which was an unthinkably abrupt way to speak to an actual member of the golf club.

He looked up from his magazine. 'Oh I had to I turn it off – it was just getting too bloody miserable,' and returned to his golf magazine while half-watching the golf scores come in.

It dawned on me then that I had to get out of there. It was no use waiting for opportunities to present themselves – I needed to see the real world.

It was time for my dessert trolley to wheel me somewhere new.

6

Acting

As I turned eighteen, I was unbearable. Reading back over my diaries, I was really pushing my Noël Coward obsession to the limits by using words like 'terribly' and 'wonderfully' all the time to ridiculous effect. 'It was terribly nice to go with Mother to Homebase to buy a new laundry basket – it matched the microwave wonderfully.' Reading it all back, it seems so phoney.

I had drive, ambition and confidence, but at the same time I had absolutely no idea what I was doing and no idea where I was going. It was like I was sitting in the driving seat of a car but couldn't work out how to take the handbrake off. This is true as an analogy, but truer if I'd actually been able to drive – learning how to operate a car felt like the sort of thing other people did.

I think I was choosing to play a part because I was too scared to work out who I actually was. Presenting a façade assuming no one will see through feels at best foolish and at worst disingenuous. I can only assume that I was determined to do things in this wilfully old-fashioned way because it was *my* way and that gave me the illusion of control, as I didn't seem able to control much in my life at this point.

I was, at the time, far too scared to take the next logical step for any young person leaving school and go to university. A lot of my friends were going and my dad was desperate for me to be the first person in our family to go. He had been encouraging me to go since I was about seven – pleading with me every time I mentioned wanting to be a performer by telling me the Two Ronnies (heroes of mine at that point) met at university (which they didn't).

I knew, though, that I couldn't go, mainly because of fear. It would be like the terror of starting secondary school all over again. I had only just gathered some semblance of being comfortable and that had taken me years, so I wasn't about to abandon that to start all over again. I kept hearing stories about how much fun it was, how the first year was just getting drunk and you didn't really do any work, but back then, fun and drinking were anathema to me.

I was irritated that people around me couldn't see how difficult this would be. Also I had no idea how I would pay for it because even the fantasist I was, I knew you couldn't just live in a flat somewhere with no money – the six hundred pounds I'd saved from the golf club would only last me so long.

More than this, I still felt like I couldn't leave my parents. It wasn't that I didn't think I could cope, I just had this deep-rooted sense that they wouldn't cope without me. If I'd asked them, I'm sure they'd have been only too glad to get rid of me – your progeny criticising your cushions all the time must start to wear thin after a while. But for some reason, I felt very strongly though that if I left home to go gallivanting in Leeds or Manchester, attend a seminar, get drunk and put a traffic cone on a statue, I'd be visited by some sort of divine punishment and both my parents would be dead.

'You'll meet all sorts of interesting people – it'll be great for you,' my teachers would reassure me. They didn't realise the complexity; what if these new and interesting people didn't like me, or much worse, what if I met people the same as me?

Also, sadly, I'd lost any love I'd had for school work.

I was totally uninspired by all my subjects – English literature seemed to be one long Jane Austen novel (namely *Mansfield Park,* where all the characters were looking for Fanny – like so many stories I've endured since). If it wasn't Austen, it was Shakespeare, and this just added another secret I had to keep hidden, which was that I couldn't understand a word of it.

It's a limitation that's persisted throughout my life that as soon as a Shakespeare play starts, the actors may as well be pompously shouting in Latin, like a British person in the 1970s shouting at a Spanish waiter. To compound my incomprehension, any Shakespeare audience seems to love and understand everything being said and laughs loudly at any of the five-hundred-year-old jokes. Whenever I've found myself in such an audience, I have always tried so hard to understand what's going on – like a dog trying to understand when its owner explains that they're going to the supermarket but won't be long. Failing to make head nor tail, I zone out, fall asleep and then hate myself for not being better at understanding.

At school, there could be no question of Shakespeare's literary superiority, even when you don't understand him – 'He is the greatest writer ever! His use of language, it is undeniable!'

'But—'

'No "buts"!'

I had no idea what to do next with my life. I couldn't go back to working at the golf club – a wheel had fallen off the dessert trolley.

Earlier in the year, sensing that everything was getting a bit humdrum for me, one of my drama teachers had suggested I audition for something called the National Youth Theatre. I applied for an audition which, having filled in a form and sent off a postal order for ten pounds, I was told would take place on the Holloway Road – a place which was the polar opposite to the safety of Bromley. In fact, when I got out at Holloway Road Tube station, a man was walking ahead of me on the pavement and his trousers fell down. Rather than stopping to pick them up and hurrying away mortified, he just carried on walking, waddling through the rest of his day. Something like this would never happen in Bromley.

The National Youth Theatre was run by a very kind man called Ed Wilson – a Geordie in his fifties, around my height and with a determined sense of humour. Beneath a witty and acerbic exterior, he was a hugely generous man who encouraged the talents of Chiwetel Ejiofor, Matt Smith, Jessica Hynes, Daniel Craig and Rafe Spall amongst many others. I had never met anyone like him before.

At this point, after years of practice, I believed wholeheartedly I was masking my sexuality completely. My choice of audition monologues however – another of Alan Bennett's *Talking Heads* ('A Chip in the Sugar' about a closeted man who lives with his mother) and a speech from Noël Coward's *Present Laughter* (in which lead character Garry Essendine proclaims 'there's far too much nonsense talked about sex') just might have given me away. I can't be sure.

I was probably the twelfth closeted gay teenager from the suburbs to perform exactly this combination of monologues that afternoon to Ed. These choices were like a silent dog whistle to other outsiders. Ed heard us and perhaps knowing what we were going through from his own experience, smiled knowingly, offered words of encouragement about our performance and thanked us for coming in before bidding us a fond farewell.

He had by this time created an organisation that embodied the notion that if you brought young people to work together, regardless of social background, race, gender, sexuality, where they were from, how they identified or what they were going through, you would be doing good.

Some weeks later an A4 envelope arrived, which clearly had more than one page inside, and to my amazement they gave me a place. I couldn't believe it. Thousands of people audition up and down the country each year, and I was chosen to be one of the lucky ones – I was finally going to be part of something. I was invited to take part in a three-week course in Tufnell Park. There was an offer to stay in student accommodation but I knew I couldn't – I'd stay at home and commute, that way I wouldn't be stuck there if I hated it.

The new chapter I had been waiting for my entire early-adult life had arrived. This National Youth Theatre course started with twenty-five teenagers gathering in a dusty room at the top of the London Metropolitan University on Holloway Road.

Despite the trepidation about meeting everyone, I felt like I could handle it if I just kept myself to myself and did things on my terms – I didn't have to talk to anyone if I didn't want to, it was fine to be on my own at lunchtime if I couldn't find anyone to talk to and if I really hated the whole experience, I could just leave. The Tube was only across the road – I just had to follow the man with no trousers.

Any theatre workshop I've encountered involves three things: spending *ages* standing in a circle ('neutrally' hands by your sides, feet shoulder width apart), 'balancing the space' (basically walking around the room) and 'rolling through the spine' (flopping forward and then really slowly coming back up to standing). I always seemed to do this faster than the rest of the group and then had to deceitfully go back down and start again, thus jolting my neck and probably undoing all the good work.

I imagine there are whole drama schools who get by making people do this for three years alongside the occasional game of something apparently essential to all actors: the game Zip Zap Boing. Zip Zap Boing is where you stand in a circle and pass the 'energy' with your hands by swinging from one side to the other and shouting, '*Zip!*' If you want to change direction, you swing the other way and shout, '*Zap!*' and if you want to bounce it across the circle at someone, you shout, '*Boing!*' It did cross my mind that this might not be such an essential part of theatre – I wondered how long John Gielgud must have played Zip Zap Boing before he got up to play Hamlet. However, it took my mind away from feeling too self-conscious about being the only person in the workshop wearing a suit, and I suppose that is exactly what all these exercises were actually designed for.

Over three weeks, this group of young people between sixteen and nineteen all worked together, and since none of us knew each other from before, we were all on an equal footing. Due to the serene, almost hippieish, ethos of the course, everyone respected one another. Normally, I'd find it very threatening to be around so many people with the same interest as me, but this time I found myself curious.

There were people from all over the UK. Previous to this I'd only really left London to go to the Imperial War Museum at Duxford on a summer trip with the Cubs and a school history field trip where we'd gone to Ironbridge (the first bridge made of iron), which after an eternal coach journey was actually quite boring as it was literally just a bridge made of iron.

My sheltered experience in Bromley meant I'd never met someone my age from Wales and certainly not someone who flew the Welsh flag out of their bedroom window; I'd never met someone from Newcastle or Manchester, Norfolk or even Reading. They were people from beyond suburban London, people who didn't make you feel ashamed to eat a cucumber because it was too flamboyant. In fact, some of these people were actual vegetarians and they still weren't even ashamed. I'd never really met a vegetarian before except for that boy in my year who also had asthma.

As a group, we spent those three weeks getting to know each other while 'filling the space' and 'rolling through the spine' between workshops from leaders and directors on stage combat, voice and singing. It was quickly apparent that our group was made up of people who weren't ashamed to let their feelings show – they hugged when they said hello and even when they said goodbye. I thought people only hugged in films, and even then mainly films set in Italy.

This hugging felt like a challenge, not least because I didn't know what I was supposed to do with my briefcase and my umbrella – the course was full of so many new experiences. If I had been in sheltered Bromley, this open hugging culture would have seemed utterly strange to me, but I soon found that when a group of people were happy and enjoying their lives, it's hard to resist wanting to join in.

Ironically, these people didn't want me to change – they actually seemed to like me being different and celebrated my unusual ways and my clothing choices (dubbed a combination of their dads' weekend outfits and an Edwardian banker.) I was starting to feel content – happy even – about who I was, but my natural self-saboteur made sure it didn't last long.

I'd paid for the course costs out of my own money made by arduously pushing that sweet trolley around the golf-club dining room – the National Youth Theatre experience had cost me twelve pavlovas, thirty-seven custard tarts and countless rhubarb crumbles. With this in mind, I had to feel like I was improving in some way, and so I'd bother the workshop leaders about how I could improve.

The directors told me I should allow myself to fail, loosen up and let go – even challenge myself to create characters who were different to myself. This was the opposite of everything I'd learnt until this point, which was largely to avoid failure and looking foolish at all costs and try to ignore other people as much as possible. It really was a huge contrast. It was almost as though the tabloid headlines I'd read at home weren't telling the truth about the wider world after all.

The directors (we were discouraged from thinking of them as 'teachers') said positive things about the group and called the short scenes we did in the workshops 'beautiful' and 'delicious' – I'd never heard something described in those terms unless it was profiteroles or maybe Princess Diana.

We even did a workshop on 'movement' led by a woman called Heather. Heather was probably in her mid-thirties and wore bright colours, dungarees and parrot earrings in a non-ironic way. She was full of positivity, and as young people, we immediately sniffed out her wholesome kids' TV energy.

Her warm-up game, rather than Zip Zap Boing, was to get us to run into the middle of the circle one by one with great enthusiasm and say our name followed by an action that represented our personality. Then everyone in the circle would copy it. I was instantly anxious as it had taken all my might to not break out in a sweat every time someone shouted, '*Boing!*' at me, never mind creating a whole mimed action to represent my entire personality.

Heather said she'd go first to demonstrate. 'I like dancing so here's mine: *Heather!* My name's Heather!' she chirped, doing what I assume she thought looked like dancing but was basically her making the 'OK' sign with her thumbs and forefingers in front of her face. Being awful teenagers, it was no challenge for us to leap to the rudest thing imaginable – poor Heather didn't realise that waving her hands in that shape, so near her head meant that she looked like she was wanking two invisible cocks straight into her face.

The whole group instantly laughed, then remembering how important this workshop experience was, tried to stifle it but then laughed even more because everyone knows that stifled laughter is the best and most addictive kind of laughter. 'This is what I love doing!' she said innocently, repeating the action again, intensifying our strangulated squeals of laughter all the more.

Heather told us about how she usually did this exercise as part of 'Theatre in Education' workshops at rough schools and in prisons, though we all wondered how the inmates on G Wing had responded to Heather's mimed porn show delivered with all the energy of an episode of *Blue Peter*.

'I always get a very positive response.'

Poor Heather had to carry on with the rest of her meticulously planned workshop despite our constant giggling – she had us 'filling the space' but this time by walking around elbows first and then noses first to see how this 'changed' us. We were all changed, but mainly by laughing.

What the uncontrollable laughter had shown us was that we were now bonded as a group. It was the first time for me, perhaps for all of us, that we'd been surrounded by people on the same wavelength. We weren't all the same, but we'd all been the weirdos and outcasts in our schools and by some arrangement had been brought together in this dusty rehearsal room, and as we all found, confidence really grows when you see yourself reflected in the people around you. It was what Heather would have called 'validating' and 'powerful'.

It was the first time I'd found myself just going with the flow without the need to question, subvert or control it by behaving like an uptight Victorian. Finally, I didn't have to explain myself. I was realising I wasn't obliged to hate myself all the time and it was OK to feel positive about not just me but those around me too. These two things tend to go hand in hand and explains why we should pity mean-spirited people because their horribleness is just a projection of how they're feeling about themselves.

Words like 'validating' and 'powerful' were words I could never have used in Bromley – they were the sort of words the *Daily Mail* might pour scorn over as though they somehow made a mockery of the sacrifices of people who fought in the Second World War and people wouldn't need to be 'validated' if they brought back National Service.

I was still making the two-hour journey to Bromley every night and bitterly regretted my decision not to stay in the halls of residence. For the first time, I really wanted to be part of the group and not sat on the outside looking in.

You might assume that with teenagers all thrown together in an open-minded liberal environment that everyone would be having sex and feeling very confident and positive (like in one of those films that lies about how great it is to be young). Perhaps everyone *was* having sex; I had no idea as I was busy getting the train back to my mum and dad's with my briefcase and my blazer.

There were about three confident boys who'd already come out, but I did not fancy them. Logically, perhaps I should have done because finally I was meeting people with the same interests as me – flamboyant outsiders who were also into guys – we'd surely have so much to talk about. We could have drawn some strength from speaking about how we were feeling, but for me, this was unthinkable. When I wasn't pretending to be Noël Coward, I was doing everything I could to avoid looking at myself. In these other gay and bisexual teenagers, who seemed so proud and true to themselves, I saw a reflection of me. A reflection of everything I'd trained myself to repress.

There's a long tradition of gay men loving unattainable straight men (basically the opposite of some of Judy Garland's life choices). I think it's a result of our first crushes being on the other boys at school who were (as the law of averages have pervaded) probably straight, combined with so many of the men we see in films and television portrayed as straight men too. I think there might also have been a sense for me that if I fancied people who didn't fancy me back, I'd always be safe from having to actually experience the vulnerability of a relationship – the conflict of loving someone and being loved back in return – especially when I'd spent so long disliking so many parts of myself.

So, I was drawn, naturally, to one straight member of the group more than others. His name was Xander and he was my age and from Norfolk. He had a friendly, smiley face, dark hair and he dressed like he was in a band – in terms of things in common, there was absolutely no reason for me to have a crush on him, but, for whatever reason, I did.

Maybe it's because he was liberal-minded – his mum taught glass blowing, the most brittle of all the crafts – and he was always nice about everyone and everything. I'd never met a boy like this (boys weren't allowed to be confident and nice in Bromley for fear of being called 'gay'), which also made me double down on my shame for fancying him – *How can you be thinking such selfish thoughts about fancying him when he's just being nice to you?* my mind blazed.

Whenever we played Zip Zap Boing, I'd gravitate towards him, except sometimes some clumsy member of the group would get in my way. On those occasions I'd have to make do with spying on him out of the corner of my eye as he stood next to that awful girl Monica from Whitstable, who always shouted, 'Boing!' and then laughed too much.

After our long days of drama exercises and mimed hand gestures, I'd hang out with the rest of the group at their halls of residence/sex palace. By the entrance was a bar for 'hanging out' and occasionally Tanya from Cleethorpes would get drunk and set up an arm-wrestling competition or punch a boy or kick over a table, and everyone thought she was great fun. Though, on reflection, she probably should have spoken to a therapist.

I would sit on the grass outside with a very restrained Coca-Cola, talking with the more serious members of our group about very meaningful topics like how a theatre was probably 'the most sacred place on Earth' and wouldn't it be great if improv workshops could be provided in war zones. Sure, we were wankers, but it was our first time not feeling weird, and I suppose you could say we were running with it.

One night, I remember everyone else gradually going inside until it was just Xander and I on the grass next to each other. We talked for ages about the world and art (I knew nothing and still know nothing about art), and we sat there, legs outstretched, almost touching, looking up at the stars. If nothing else, at eighteen I had a great eye for a filmic, romantic setting, and I seemed obsessed with looking at the night sky.

Xander's polite conversation made me mistake his niceness for potentially being gay, and so my mission became clear – I would somehow ask him to be my boyfriend. He seemed to enjoy sitting on the grass with me, and we talked for what seemed like hours. As I wasn't staying at the halls of residence, I needed somewhere to put my briefcase so naturally I asked Xander if I could leave it in his room – asking a favour of him seemed like the best first step in engaging him in my life.

As Xander and I came back inside from our long stargazing chat, Whitstable Monica was there waiting by the door, presumably to entrap Xander in some boring gossip about what Diane or Graham had said to Tanya so she didn't punch them. 'Sounds like a really cruel way of making fun of people actually,' I said to Monica, piously.

Later, Xander and her seemed to be talking for ages at the bar. *Won't she ever let him go?!* I mused, *Doesn't she realise we all just want to catch up with each other, not get locked in boring one-on-ones?* ignoring the fact that this was exactly what I'd done with Xander earlier. Pride meant I didn't want to seem desperate, so I went to make sure I had long chats with everyone else

– loudly and with lots of laughter about arm wrestling and Tanya punching people.

I looked around the bar and suddenly realised Xander and Monica had left. I was perturbed that he would have taken her to our special stargazing place and ran outside to check, suddenly aware that I didn't have much time to make it across London for my last train back to Bromley.

They weren't outside, which was a huge relief, but then it dawned on me it was much worse and that if they weren't downstairs, they must be upstairs, maybe in his room. Presumably together. Apart from the hurt of thinking of them together, I needed to get my briefcase. I galloped up the stairs two at a time to Xander's room and knocked on the door. There was no response, but I was sure they were in there.

It wasn't just about the bag at this point – it was about so much more. What was Whitstable Monica playing at? We all had to be at a clowning workshop at ten o'clock the next morning and really this was a terrible waste of time for Xander, who surely just wanted to get some sleep and reflect on our insightful chat about how if the army was turned into theatre practitioners we wouldn't need wars any more.

Obviously, on some level, I knew I wanted to sabotage them. I berated myself for being so stupid – it was like Michael and the fish knives all over again. Being straight seemed so easy – there was so much choice, and if you just chatted in the bar you then went upstairs together while little gays like me had to travel through the centuries and back again to try to find someone to even sit on the grass and look at the stars.

Hearing no reply, I decided to put the mockers on this teenage knocking shop, and with a deep breath, I burst through the door. To my abject horror, they were both sat there on the bed, fully clothed, in what looked to me like a very intimate chat, seen in the light of the overhead bulb, which they'd left on – I was equally appalled that they had no idea about the importance of mood lighting and had ignored the bedside lamp.

'I have just come to get my bag,' I announced in the doorway. I grabbed my briefcase. 'Sorry!' I shouted as I ran away.

I realised I now had to dash to get the Tube. The exercise ran off the adrenaline, pounding the pavement, briefcase flailing, through those dark streets, the tall Victorian house façades glaring down at me judgementally, knowing that I'd deliberately tried to sabotage Xander's tryst with Whitstable Monica. It was like I was becoming addicted to disappointment, and it was turning into a perverse will to try to sabotage other people's happiness.

Sat at last on my train back to the quiet suburbs, I felt like I was a million miles away from the glamour of the halls of residence where Xander was. The electricity of the moment faded now to the dull thud of knowing someone you liked didn't like you back and, to make matters worse, he was in that very moment with someone else.

At this point, my only points of reference for matters of the heart were the occasional gay TV dramas like *Tinsel Town* and the film *Beautiful Thing,* which, like so many dramas since, suggested to me that if you take the step of coming out to someone, they'll probably fall in love with you and then you'd have a relationship and everything would be just great. Or even if it wasn't great and you eventually break up horribly, at least you'd had that moment when someone said they liked you back.

So that was my mission: I'd tell Xander how I felt and that would lead to us falling in love, even though he was displaying

all the hallmarks of being straight, and indeed, fancying someone else. I'd known that at some point I'd probably have to
come out, and now it would be worth all the awkwardness if I
finally had someone to love (even though I was still failing to
grasp that he was displaying distinctly straight tendencies).
Now, in order to keep up with my lust for romantic settings, I
just needed to find a perfect time to get him on his own to tell
him.

That weekend, I suggested we go to a matinée, and Xander
said he'd never seen *Blood Brothers*. Despite knowing my way
round London from visiting all those vintage-clothing markets,
I deliberately got us lost so we missed the start of the show.
'Oh no! You were so looking forward to it too!' I said,
deceitfully.

'Yeah, I just wanted to see a show,' he said, disappointed. I
felt a pang of guilt that I'd manipulated the situation so easily.
The guilt was fleeting though because Xander was about to be
treated to the most wonderful matinée in all of London.

We started walking down Charing Cross Road, past the
antique bookshops. I could feel my heart rate quickening,
preparing myself for the performance of a lifetime. He started
blathering on about wanting to do a gap year where he did
drama workshops in rural Africa. I quickly shut him up.

'Xander, can I tell you something? It's a bit awkward'

'Yeah, course, Tom – is it about *Blood Brothers*? Because I
didn't want to see it that much anyway.'

'No it's not about musicals, well, not really. I'm . . .. I'm . . .
I'm homosexual.'

Homosexual – even my choice of word seemed like I'd
plumped for the most formal, least emotional option. I may as
well have reeled off a load of 1950s euphemisms: 'I'm light in

my loafers! I bat for the other team! I'm a friend of Dorothy!' All of which would have sounded like nonsense to Xander.

Regardless, I had at last done it – this deadweight I'd carried around inside, the source of so much shame and misery finally out in the open. The exhaustion of keeping it hidden was over, and judgmental Bromley had at last been vanquished. I was allowed to be a person with feelings, who loved and didn't need to feel ashamed about it. Real life could finally begin.

'Oh, Tom. Right . . . OK . . . Well, thanks for telling me. I'm not gay, but I can imagine that was a tough thing to say.' And then there was a pause. 'Actually, my uncle's gay.'

What? I didn't want a rundown of his family history. I wanted to scream, 'Oh great your uncle's gay – I've got a second cousin who moved to Birmingham but I don't see how this is relevant now.'

The TV dramas had lied. I wasn't embarking on some hugely validating relationship with sex and everything thrown in. All I was embarking on was an awkward walk down Charing Cross Road, feeling hot and embarrassed and knowing something about my crush's uncle. I wished we'd just gone to see *Blood Brothers* after all.

In the cold light of that afternoon, the nonsense fantasy I'd created in my mind came crashing down around me and I felt ashamed that I'd ever thought he'd fancy me. I was too uptight anyway in my blazer and smart shoes, looking like a geography teacher but acting like a silly kid playing kiss-chase in the playground. I wonder if this is how a lot of gay young people feel – kept hopelessly naïve because we can't develop any emotional maturity like the straight kids do in the playground, having to feel so grown-up and self-reliant because we're used to keeping secrets from the people around us.

Since I was too scared to talk to the other gays around me, I had no way of knowing.

Xander went off to meet the rest of the group at Pizza Hut, but I wasn't in the mood. The last thing I needed after the failure of the bravest thing I'd ever done was a stuffed crust and a salad bar.

I was feeling confused. Some of the promised lightness once you tell someone was there, but since Xander didn't feel the same, I just felt guilty for burdening him with the information. There was no guidance on what might happen next – perhaps he would tell his uncle.

I felt so guilty about making him miss the matinée that I bought Xander a gift to say thanks for listening – a book of Shakespearean sonnets. Itself too obvious as a gift, too laden with meaning, but I knew Xander loved Shakespeare, so it felt like a suitably serious gift. The fact that I zoned out as soon as anyone spoke in iambic pentameter should have been a sign that it could never work out. We never mentioned that afternoon again.

When the course ended, we were all very sad to say goodbye and promised we'd stay in touch forever and la la la. Back in Bromley in my bedroom later that night, I burst into tears for the first time since I was ten. Crying as an adult is very different to when you're a child; it's not the sort of instant response to falling over when there's shock and pain and embarrassment, a primal shout for help. As an adult, I didn't know what it was as it felt more like a shaking sensation that started in my chest and crept up onto my face. But it was silent, which was ideal as it meant there was no risk of my parents hearing.

Now the course was finished, there was nothing to fill my diary; I had no university place to go to, no job and no gap year planned. I'd gone from model student to unemployed in one afternoon.

I tried to cheer myself up by finding some ribbons I kept for my elaborate present-wrapping rituals and put them round my mirror. It felt like the sort of thing my creative friends from the course would do – express yourself! Adorn your life with things you like! Celebrate! Colours! Ribbons! Yeah! Dad looked less impressed when he came to tell me dinner was ready.

I think the course had taught me a lot about acting and given me a glimpse of the wider world, but I realise now I didn't really want to be an actor at all. It turned out, I was just gay.

7

Travelling

Things never seem to go the way they do in films and on television; they don't go the way other people make them go, the way I'm sure they should go. For example, while friends of mine went on gap years, getting to know themselves in Thailand and Vietnam, making friends, taking drugs and getting bar jobs in Australia, I managed to find myself with an aunt (actually not a real aunt but another friend of my mum) and her mother-in-law in the suburbs just outside Providence, Rhode Island. The potential to go on an adventure round Asia was deemed far too dangerous by my mother, who said I'd be kidnapped and have my organs stolen.

I always had dreams of travelling and writing a diary like Hemingway or, of course, Noël Coward, but with the modest wage earned pushing a dessert trolley round a golf course, I think the first-class comforts I dreamed of were always going to be off-limits. 'Do you *want* to be sleeping in a youth hostel in Cambodia and get all your things stolen? Including your organs? Do you? Do you?' asked Mum. I can't imagine anyone would possibly say yes to this question. 'Because if you do, then that's exactly where you should go!'

So, I decided to go to the USA. Like anyone who was a child in the eighties and nineties, I dreamed about America. I painted pictures of the Manhattan skyline obsessively and tried to play *Rhapsody in Blue* on the piano (the loud bits, anyway) and by extension I loved reading about the Roaring Twenties – *The Great Gatsby* and also *The Great Gatsby*. Being very busy with my A-Levels, I thought one book was more than enough.

Also, it seemed there was less chance of organ theft in America because everyone was apparently so wealthy as we'd seen on our screens in *Home Alone* and also my mum's friend Mary lived in a small town just outside Providence and, though she was in her fifties, there was a feeling that she'd be able to defend me if the need arose. How rife organ theft in any part of the world was at that time is unclear – I don't remember it ever being mentioned in the news, for example.

This was the first time I'd been away – and certainly the first time I'd been on a plane – on my own. I was convinced that I would be absolutely fine, much as I was still convinced that I had been born as a forty-six-year-old. My flight with US Airways was booked through a travel agent and my plane ticket was printed on paper and placed in a navy-blue wallet. As I said thank you and goodbye to the travel agents, I imagine they immediately threw their typewriters out of the window, picked up their shoulder bags and turned the sign on the door to *Closed* for the final time as they must have been the last travel agents to exist in the whole world.

Mum and Dad gave me a lift to the airport (of course), and Mum got tearful saying goodbye, even though I was only going for two and a half weeks. It is a design flaw in airports that they have snaking lines to go through security, so once you've said your tearful goodbye and walked off, you then have to walk past your loved ones again as the line snakes back round, thus starting the tears off all over again.

In spring 2002, it was barely six months after 9/11 and I didn't know you were now forbidden from taking sharp objects in your hand luggage in case you tried to hijack the plane by threatening to cut the pilot's cuticles. Like any eighteen-year-old, I was horrified at having my manicure set removed from my bag by the security guards. Still adjusting to this strict new protocol themselves, they allowed me to walk back to Mum and Dad, who had stopped crying just long enough for me to hand it to them for safe keeping before Mum immediately started crying again.

On the plane, I was finally out in the world on my own – my big adventure, my chance to be an adult, free from other people's judgement and that nagging feeling in suburbia that I wasn't quite right.

Aunty Mary had been a school friend of my mum when she lived in Sydenham. In the 1970s she went on a cruise and when it docked in America she, as Dad would say, 'copped for a Yank' (married an American), who sadly died not long after their two daughters were born. She'd brought them both up single-handed. They lived in Florida now and during mum's annual phone call to her, she enquired if I might be able to go over and stay in their room. Aunty Mary said she'd be delighted to have me at her home in Rhode Island.

Before the internet took off, there was no easy way to find a photograph of someone – there was no social media, for example – so I landed in America, my first time away from home, looking for a woman I'd never seen before except in Mum's photographs from the 1960s. So I hastily looked round for a woman in a big skirt and a beehive hair-do.

'There you are!' said a fifty-year-old woman with grey hair swept back into a bun and kooky glamorous glasses, standing next to a stout and serious man with dark hair.

'Mary . . . ?'

'Ahh, I found you!'

'Hello!' I shouted, hugging her and then hugging the man next to her. There followed an awkward pause before Mary explained that she didn't know him – he was just someone she'd asked for directions to the arrivals hall.

'Bob! It's so great to finally meet you – you made it to America!'

This felt exciting, but I didn't know why she'd just called me Bob. We finally walked out of the terminal and the cool spring air hit me, the first fresh air I'd felt for hours, though it was tainted with the smell of cinnamon and bacon that taints every-thing in America. However, I was there, in the United States, albeit in a multistorey car park outside an airport, but still, I was there.

'I haven't got a fancy car, Bob, so don't go thinking I've got a Lincoln Town Car or nothing – it's just a normal Ford!' she said with a laugh.

'It's a lovely car! Thanks ever so much for coming to pick me up,' I said, buckling up in Mary's sporty hatchback.

'I couldn't have you making your own way,' said Mary, sounding almost outraged. 'I've been excited about you coming over. Shall we go get a nice slice of pizza, Bob?'

'Yeah sure!' I said, ignoring the fact that she seemed to have immediately forgotten my name but still so excited to have something so American almost the moment I stepped off the plane.

An hour later, Mary swung the Ford into the empty park-ing lot in front of the pizza place like a rally driver and screeched to a halt. 'OK, Bob, we're here.' She clambered out of the car.

'Oh, cheers! Cheers!' said the man behind the counter in a fake London accent, smiling and trying to be British as we collected our huge pizza boxes. 'And sorry to hear about the Queen Mom.'

'Cheers!' I said merrily as we took our dinner to eat in the car. The pizza box had an enormous American flag across it since 9/11 had upped the prevalence of flag waving in a nation famous for loving its Stars and Stripes so much that children already had to make promises to it.

Mary explained further, in the orange glow of the car light. 'It used to be people would say to you, "Oh, I'm Irish," because their great-great-grandfather had come over from Ireland in 1800-and-whatever, but after 9/11, ask anyone where they're from – America!'

'But on the pizza boxes? Do they need to be reminded of where they are from even when they ordered a takeaway – I mean a pizza is Italian!'

'I know, Bob – that's just what they do here. They love flags on everything.'

But it's like us having a Chinese takeaway with a picture of the Queen on it, I thought to myself, too polite to say out loud.

'Oh, Bob,' said Mary, flinging the pizza boxes into the bin from the car window. 'Do you mind if we make a stop to see my mother-in-law, Thelma? She's in the geriatric home. She's so negative about everything, it gets me down, you know? But I have to go and see her – she was good to me when I moved here. You know my husband, Gabe? He was a keen sportsman – as fit as a flea, and then one day he just dropped dead. Dropped dead! That was it! I had my two girls and I had to do my best for them, you know? Thelma was very good to me during all of that.'

'Sure . . .' It wasn't what I had in mind for my first adventure as an adult – a visit to a nursing home – but it was an outing nonetheless, and since Aunty Mary was having me to stay, I wanted to be polite, and apart from anything else I liked running errands. 'By the way, erm, thank you for having me to stay – but I'm actually Tom, not Bob.'

'What?' There was an awkward pause and I suddenly panicked that I'd got in the wrong car. 'Oh, I know – I call everyone that! It's short for '*bobbeleh*'. Gabe, he was Jewish, and everyone calls everyone 'bobbeleh'. It just means 'dear' or 'darling' – it's Yiddish – so, 'Bob' for short!'

I'd already learnt from Aunty Jilly (who's another person who's not actually my aunty but my mum's best friend from when she worked in The Army & Navy and who is Jewish) that it's pronounced 'b*u*bbeleh', but before I could point this out, we arrived at the old folks' home. I think Aunty Mary might have learnt her Yiddish while still trying to learn her American accent, so she ended up sounding like she was from South London and New England all at once.

'Bob!' Thelma exclaimed as we walked in to her room at the nursing home – I guess in America I was always going to be Tom but also Bob.

'How are you, Thelma?' asked Mary.

'Terrible – I hate it here. There's nothing to do and I hate the television.' Mary hadn't lied about the negativity. Not that I could blame her – it didn't feel like a very fabulous place. Suddenly another resident of the home came in, waltzing on her own, speaking what sounded like Russian while seeming to dust Thelma's chest of drawers. She kept speaking, imploring us to answer, confused that we didn't know how. 'I can't understand any more than you do – hide my pearls, would you, dear?' whispered Thelma from her wheelchair. I put them in a drawer while Mary called the nurse to remove the dancing lady. 'They're all like that in here. Enjoy your life, Bob – you'll end up here sooner than you know,' said Thelma. 'I can't even get out of bed on my own,' she said, clicking her dentures. 'I tried the other week and fell over. Now they're punishing me by making me go to bed early and I have to be supervised for six weeks.'

'OK, dear. We've got to go. Tom's exhausted – he just got off his flight from London!' Mary wrapped up.

'Who's Tom?'

'Come on, Bob' said Mary.

'Bye, Bob.' said Thelma as I made a little bow to her, 'Oh, Mary, he's a perfect English gentleman!'.

We drove back to Mary's condo in a leafy corner of the leafiest corner of Rhode Island. The roads were wider and homes more spaced out with their mailboxes on the edge of their lawns, but ultimately, it was the same place I'd just left; it was Bromley with a different accent. Lying in bed in Mary's spare room, I felt a mixture of excitement and a nagging feeling that seeing Thelma in the nursing home was a sign that I should grab life by the horns and live it right now. I had to live every moment because you might be in a nursing home sooner than you know.

I wrote in my diary that Mary's home was 'immaculate, and decorated in the best taste with mirrored furniture, lots of white and cream, thick carpet and no clutter, but I don't like her Bauhaus conical kettle'. I was no Hemingway, but I was already showing signs of being a judgey little bitch. My approach to 'grabbing life by the horns' was apparently to give a review of the soft furnishings – roughing it in a youth hostel in Cambodia probably would have killed me.

The next day, Mary took me to her office in Providence, where she answered phones for a construction firm because they loved her English accent. Though, to be honest, her Sydenham- Rhode Island-mid-Atlantic accent was sort of from nowhere and everywhere in between.

'Bob, meet Marcy, who I job share with on the front desk. Marcy, this is my nephew!'

Marcy seemed to be a joyless woman in her late twenties. She was sitting very upright with her legs entwined tightly underneath the reception desk. Wearing a grey sweater and her hair in tight brown curls, she had a facial expression that managed to look blank and terrified all at the same time, like the whole world was just full of unpleasant surprises.

'Well, you know it's Bring Your Daughters to Work Day today, Mary? Not bring your nephews to work?' Marcy piped up, trying to make a joke, but since it appeared that she never smiled, it just sounded like we were being told off or that she was a robot.

'Haha, no, I didn't, Marcy!' said Mary, laughing at this joke as she bustled to hang up her coat on the hat stand behind the desk.

'We just love your Aunt Mary here – she's so British and so proper!' and then apropos of nothing, 'Would you like to see my acting portfolio?'

I hadn't mentioned that I was interested in theatre and had dreams of being an actor myself, because I'd only walked in the door forty-five seconds ago, so this gave me the sense that Marcy might proffer this book to literally everyone if they stood still for long enough. 'What?' I responded. 'Er, yes . . .'

In a well-practised manoeuvre, she reached under the desk to produce, with no small amount of effort, a large folder and immediately started displaying the laminated pages on the reception desk. Images of Marcy looking her trademark blank-terrified in upbeat productions of *Calamity Jane*, *The Sound of Music* and *Godspell*. She had a face perfect for her role as, I assumed, some sort of beggar in *Les Mis* but less so for her role in *Sweet Charity*. '. . . I hoped it would lead to some more real acting work, but it's so difficult to get attention outside of the major cities,' she said. It did seem ambitious to try to get a casting director from Hollywood to travel three thousand miles to see you, especially when you only had two facial expressions.

'Bob, quick!' Mary interrupted suddenly. 'They just had a meeting in the conference room. You should go help yourself to the food left over.'

'Oh, I'm fine, thank you'.

'No, Bob, go get some – it's only going to waste!'

'But I don't want anything, I'm not hungry—'

'Bob!'

'Mary!'

'OK, Bob, I just don't want you to go hungry, that's all!'

'Your Aunty Mary just wants to look after everyone,' called Marcy from under the desk as she put her acting portfolio away (and not for the last time that day, I'm sure) .

The rain cleared in the afternoon – it was finally my time to explore and be free. It was what I'd been saving for, what I'd travelled all this way for – my time to be my own man, in America, the land of the free!

'Come back round five thirty, Bob. Then we can get the train home?'

'Sure.' I was basically living my Bromley life but with higher buildings.

Staying in a city as a tourist with no purpose other than to 'see' things is at first exciting, and then quite overwhelming, and then, in my experience, quite boring. I looked around a couple of old houses open to the public. It was interesting in that there were things to see, some of which were over two hundred years old but like so many historical buildings around the world, each one was really just another house full of chairs and tables and, well, things. I did what the other visitors did and took photos and read the placards and listened to the guides who were all very knowledgeable and enthusiastic.

With any monument though, especially if it's a famous one, despite your hopes that visiting it will yield some transcendent moment, it becomes like anything in life – you just look at it, take a photo and then move on. Maybe there's a placard next to it, but it doesn't change you; it's just a thing, in a world of loads of things.

This was in the time before you could see the photo immediately on the camera, and long before you could take a photo to show off on social media – the photo itself was just a dull click and then a long wait of several weeks before the photo was taken to a chemist or photographic shop to be developed. Everything felt like it was waiting to happen.

The next day, Mary said we were going on a special trip to the Las Vegas of the Eastern Seaboard – Atlantic City. Finally, I was going to see some of the glamour America had to offer. Mary had an errand to run there, even though it was a very long drive away – she needed to use up a credit note for a women's boutique. Even now I love running errands because they give me a sense of purpose – almost as though I have a job, but unlike a job there is always time to chat to people, look around and notice the views.

For British people brought up watching the opulent home lives of Americans in films like *Home Alone* and, in my case, *The Golden Girls* it was surprising to see that when the sun goes behind the clouds, a lot of American towns look just like Croydon. Atlantic City was no different except it had a view of the ocean, so it was more like Margate or Clacton. Skipping past the vast, faded casinos with their water features and naked Roman gods beaming down at us, Mary said, 'Do you know what I'd hate, Bob?'

'No.'

'To be buried alive – wouldn't that be terrible?'

'Oh sure.'

We went to the small women's clothing store on a side street leading down to the boardwalk. Independent women's 'boutiques' like this seem to always have a hotchpotch of eye-catching outfits that I've never seen anyone wear: denim all-in-ones with sequined ticks on one arm or a row of rhinestones across the top of a pocket next to evening dresses draped off haunting mannequins awkward and severe in their poses. Wearing cock-angled wigs shaped into grey bobs, their arms point open-handed at the floor, woefully, or gesticulate at the heavens like the chorus in a Greek tragedy, declaiming they'd already seen far, far too much. It's hard to imagine who would see a display like this and think, *Yes – yes, that's what I want to look like.*

A small bell rang as we pushed the door, and a woman with orange skin and what looked like several facelifts immediately greeted us, her skin pulled tight underneath her eyes and around her mouth. 'How can I help you today?' she said brightly, but in a way that suggested she'd never been happy.

'Oh, yes,' said Mary positively. 'I've got a credit note I'd like to redeem as it expires soon.'

The shop assistant's face dropped, (which would no doubt be an expensive repair). This was a non-sale, a waste of her time. 'I'll get Michael,' she said coldly.

Michael appeared through the beaded curtain and stood behind the glass counter – his altar, under which were huge costume jewellery pieces that looked like they'd walked straight off the set of *Dynasty*. Earrings larger than a person's hand, necklaces thicker than a person's wrist. Michael, like his assistant, was also orange but had a gravelly voice achieved presumably from a lifetime of smoking. Mary was already bustling around and tugging at a denim jumpsuit with a tied denim belt and contrasting, but still denim, collar.

'Oh, that's outstanding!' he rasped, as she exited the small changing cubicle. 'If I were wearing this, I'd tie it – just tie it – oh excuse me – tie it, I mean, I'm not doing this properly,' he said, faffing with denim. 'If I was doing this properly – oh but yes – yes – it's stunning.' I'd never seen such a performance over a belt.

'Where are you from – you've got an accent?' he enquired, rounding on me accusingly.

'I'm from London.'

'London, huh? You must be so sad about the Queen Mom – she just died, right?'

'Right . . .'

'Do you think she killed Diana?'

Before I had a chance to answer Mary reappeared triumphantly from the tiny changing cubicle and announced. 'I've got a credit note to pay for this – that OK, right?'

'Sure, I can do that – can I see it?'

Mary scrabbled around in her shoulder bag. 'Here you go.'

Michael looked down to scan the note. 'Oh, I can't accept this – it's from 1998. I'm sorry, I can't accept it this far down the line.' He held it out for her to take back.

Mary suddenly upped her game. 'Excuse my French, but that's horse shit – you can take it now as you could take it then. What's the year got to do with it?' I did think that four years was quite a long time ago – it wasn't unreasonable of Michael to question it. A long pause ensued. Mary wasn't going to back down; even if her accent had become skewed, her South London fighting spirit wasn't going anywhere. In the battle between the New Jersey Shore and Sydenham, it turned out Sydenham won. 'OK, I'll do it – but just this once'.

'I don't mean to be rude,' snipped Mary as we trotted back to the car, 'but I thought that man was an asshole, Bob. What difference does it make with the year? It's still my money he's got.'

'Sure, yeah.'

'And I know you didn't like the look of the outfit – I could see it in your eyes, Bob, but what else could I do? The credit note was *so* old!'

'Oh, I did like it! It'll be nice for wearing out at the . . . weekends.'

'I guess you're right. Now, come on, let's go get some Chinese food.' We found a restaurant with American flags on the menu and ate watching the sun set over the ocean.

I was definitely enjoying this round of errands and trips to the seaside, the city and the geriatric facilities, but despite its comforting humdrum, I felt guilty to admit it wasn't quite the adventure I thought I'd be having when I left Bromley. I had taken F. Scott Fitzgerald's *Tender is the Night* with me to read, but it didn't seem to fit. The world he described was eighty years before and long since gone. I don't remember ever reading stories about him and Zelda Charleston-ing on top of a New York cab and then going to buy a pizza with his aunt in the suburbs.

I'd come to America to see America, and that meant one thing: going to New York City. Surely, this would be the adventure I'd hoped for? The rousing opening chords of *Rhapsody in Blue* were already sounding in my ears when Aunty Mary came with me to the Greyhound bus station to start my journey. 'Be careful, Bob – take care now!' as she waved me off.

I was so excited about seeing the towering splendour in the distance. I felt like I was following in the spats of Gatsby and Nick. However, they weren't on a Greyhound bus and on their trip, it wasn't raining. None of the famous skyline was visible through the low cloud, so it was a surprise to look up and suddenly see the dense buildings as it dawned on me that I was finally there, in the city I'd dreamed about.

The West Forty-Second Street–Port Authority Bus Terminal owes nothing to the musical named after that same street, but on this particular Thursday afternoon at the end of April it was playing classical music during the rush hour. It's a trick I've since seen transport management use all over the world, I guess to calm down the tetchy, exhausted commuters and stop them from breaking out into fights when tourists like me walk too slowly because we've brought too much in our bags and we're tired.

I waited in line in the rain for a yellow taxi and eventually sat in the back of one, waiting to be asked where I'd like him to go. 'Yes?' the driver said as though I'd just sat in the back of his own personal car.

'Oh, hello, please may I go to number one thousand seven hundred and fifty-three, Twenty-Seventh street, please?' I said, trying to sound casually confident and like I spend loads of time in New York. That was the address I thought I'd read in my guidebook. There followed a pause, and I could feel the driver getting annoyed.

'Twenty-Seventh Street and what?!' I had no idea that the streets being so long, a taxi driver would have no idea where any building number was, and I quickly felt hopelessly naïve, squashing the sense that I was a grown-up who could cope with the big city.

'Where you from?' asked the driver.

'Oh, London!' I said, brightening, fully expecting some more questions about the Queen Mother.

'You just come in from there?'

'Oh no, I've been in Rhode Island.'

'Got a girlfriend?' Somehow this question made me feel uncomfortable.

'Oh no – I was just staying with my aunt—' which really should have explained all he needed to know but before I could tell him more about our adventures with a credit note and a denim one-piece, he smiled to himself.

'They have some fine women down in the island – you must've met some of the women down there?'

'Er . . .' I felt like he didn't want me to talk about elderly Thelma and Marcy, the struggling actress on reception.

'The girl I knew from the island, she was so fine – she was too good to use a rubber on. You don't want to use a rubber with a woman like that!' I was just relieved I hadn't started telling him about Aunty Mary. 'This where you wanted?' he asked abruptly, stopping outside The Gershwin, the aptly named youth hostel I'd booked a private room in.

'Yes, thank you. And thank you for the chat!' I said, flicking through my envelope of US dollars to pay him before I skipped out.

In from the rain, I showered and changed and took a moment to appreciate this space of my own, all to myself, which I'd actually paid for with my own money. A youth hostel is a cheap place to stay because usually you have a bed in a shared dormitory but even in this instance, I'd managed to subvert it by booking one of their private rooms – a further confirmation that my mother was right and I'd never have been able to slum it in a backpacker youth hostel in Cambodia. Apart from anything else, my school days had taught me I was very uncomfortable wearing a backpack.

I was ready to start my life as an independent man about town, and being in a town in which nobody knew me, my excitement grew when it dawned on me I could be whoever I wanted to be.

The rain still pouring outside, I sat in the internet café in the bright-red hostel lobby, next to the reception desk. The internet café consisted of two angular computer terminals in the corner, next to a vending machine. The computers had bar stools in front of them and a box underneath for paying for the rental of the terminal. The payment box was at a perfect height to bash your knee on, and thus all email conversations involved getting banged shins at least once during each exchange.

'Ooh, you smell nice!' said the woman on the neighbouring stool in her Kiwi accent.

'Oh, do I? Thank you!' I said politely, not sure how I should respond – the alternatives being 'Yes, I do!' and 'Oh no, that's not me'.

'Mmm, that is a nice aftershave! Wanna have dinner with me and this guy I've been hanging out with? We're going for some Italian food.' I was not used to people being so forthright and I didn't know who 'this guy' was, so felt I couldn't possibly say yes. Also I was onto them – this New Zealander was clearly after one thing, and that was stealing my organs.

Even now I don't like accepting impromptu invitations because there's always the possibility that we might not agree on the restaurant – people have different opinions and budgets after all, and maybe we'd end up going somewhere disappointing. It was my reluctance to meet up with school friends during the summer holidays all over again – what if they led me astray and made me join a gang? Besides, we might not have interests in common to talk about and the whole thing could be a disaster conversationally and, worse, a waste of one of my two nights in Manhattan! I was only just starting to enjoy having my own time and my own space.

'I'd be delighted,' I said.

'Great! We're going to meet in the lobby in thirty minutes!'

I made sure I left the hostel twenty-five minutes later to ensure I missed the meeting and prayed that I never saw her again. The rain had reduced to a drizzle but somehow my shoes were wet when I looked up and saw, brightly illuminated in front of me in an emerald-green wash, the Empire State Building. I could hear *Rhapsody in Blue* starting to play again in my head – either that or it was the background jazz of a nearby Starbucks.

'You wanna see some Rolls-Royce bitches?!' asked a big man suddenly standing at my shoulder on the sidewalk.

'No, thank you!' I said, tapping into my dad's advice about never looking like a tourist. The man followed me. He clearly couldn't see that I definitely didn't want to see any Rolls-Royce bitches, nor Bentley ones neither, nor even Mercedes bitches, and also I don't think it's very nice to call anyone a 'bitch'.

'You *know* you wanna see some Rolls-Royce bitches!'

I quickly made an about turn and jumped into Starbucks, which, at this time, was quite a new brand and seemed very glamorous as they hadn't yet branched out into motorway service stations. I sat for a while with a mocha, at a table all alone, kind of wishing I'd gone for dinner with the Kiwi girl and her friend. I realised making friends in a land of strangers was harder than I'd assumed. You can't just walk up to someone and say, 'Hello, would you like to be my friend?' because even as children the first thing we are taught is that this is exactly how perverts greet you.

This was also before phones were constantly in our hands to make us look busy and connected with people around the world at all times of the day and night. All you could do back then was stare out the window or read a book, but reading a book in public, in a café, felt like it broke a social contract. It was at this point that the man from behind the counter offered me his banana loaf (not a euphemism). 'We can't keep it beyond today. Would you like it? On the house.'

'Oh, thank you,' I said, taking a slice.

'No, no, take the whole thing – we can't keep it.'

'But wouldn't anyone else like some?'

It was at this point I realised I was the only person there. It crossed my mind that perhaps the Starbucks man was trying to be my friend, but I literally had no idea how to tell. I didn't know if I should reciprocate, suggest going to a bar or another coffee shop, though, surely, that would be a busman's holiday for him. Then it dawned on me that he was just doing his job. I'd had no training in making friends and my only social contact in this city was someone paid to be there, in a coffee shop which was about to close.

I had missed a key element in planning this trip – human interaction, and I was starting to feel lonely. After the excitement of having my own space to stay in, I was quickly realising that it can actually feel too big when you have only yourself to fill it, especially because I'd been conditioned to fear everyone. I took the banana loaf and headed back to my room.

The following day was my first experience of planning an entire day for myself, and in so many ways, I was finally getting to explore the place I'd always dreamed of, even if it was more tricky than I'd expected. A boat trip seemed to be the most logical first activity, as it would mean I'd get an overview of the island of Manhattan, and I managed to book myself on the 'full tour', which involved sitting on the top deck of a boat alongside sixty-five Italian school children while listening to a tour guide incant tedious details about buildings and then repeat them in Italian.

'To the left of the famous United Nations building, you'll see an apartment block where Barbra Streisand once lived. At one time . . .' It was fast dawning on me that bare facts are both useless and don't help you feel like you're experiencing a city. I managed to move away from the school children and sit near the back across the gangway from a woman and her two young sons.

The south side of Manhattan has all the famous buildings, but since our 'full trip' was going the whole way round the island, we soon left the interesting landmarks behind us and chugged past factories and people's uninteresting houses and apartment blocks. I regretted not researching what boat trip to take – even the tour guide gave up and sat down, facing us so we were all just sat there looking at each other like a doctor's waiting room floating on water.

'Hi, I'm Tracy, and these are my sons, Joe and Connor. We're from Springfield – where are you from?'

I was delighted to make a friend. 'Oh, London!' I said croakily, since this was my first conversation of the day.

'Wow!' she beamed, shaking my hand. 'Jeez are we glad to have you guys as our allies.' I didn't have the heart to tell her I wasn't really the fighting type. 'My husband is away on active service in the Middle East. I just thank God for Bush building up the military. We need to defend ourselves from these people.' I assumed she meant al-Qaeda, rather than boring tour guides. 'They'll stop at nothing, apparently! Oh gosh, when I think about it . . .'

I took a breath to say something – anything – to change the subject, but I was too slow; Tracy was on a roll: 'I couldn't stand that Clinton. And the sex scandal! Huge embarrassment for the US. Bush would never do that – a real leader.' Her young son, Joe, looked as though he might ask something (presumably, 'Why are we on this boring boat trip?'). 'Not now, honey, Mom's talking. Oh, and I love the Queen by the way.'

I was grateful for the company, but after two minutes with Tracy, I was exhausted and managed to quickly say my goodbyes to them as we finally skipped off the tedious boat. 'Lovely to meet you!' she shouted as she waved me off from the gangplank.

The next place on my must-see list was the Metropolitan Museum of Art. Walking past Central Park, a group of homeless men threw a beer can at me, which, if anything, felt exciting – so archetypally New York. I wasn't fazed by it, I was just desperate to see my favourite painting, the inspiration for my favourite Sondheim musical *Sunday in the Park With George*. 'Oh yes, I know it, sir. That's in Chicago' said the attendant. It was dawning on me that I really should have researched this trip beyond reading *The Great Gatsby*. 'Where's that accent from?' he asked.

'London!' I said with a bright grin. I was glad to talk to anyone and was poised to start up a chat about the Queen Mother.

'Oh,' said the attendant and walked off. Even someone whose job it was to talk to gallery visitors couldn't be bothered to talk to me – he must have smelled my desperation, that and the beer thrown at me by those homeless men.

Determined not to be beaten by my lack of friends, I decided I needed to use this new found freedom to finally explore what it was to be a young gay man without the fear of being judged by people in Bromley or worrying what would happen if I saw someone from home. According to my guidebook, the only detail about New York's gay district was that it was near Christopher Street in the West Village, so I decided to hotfoot it there. I needed to buy a new guidebook with more detail to understand where guys went. I knew I needed to meet other gay men – on my own I felt less gay and more just plain chatty.

I found the first shop with a rainbow flag outside, which in the early 2000s was one of the signals that meant 'This place has gays', and walked in. I'd never been in a shop like this before; in London their windows were always covered with black plastic which, while adding to the mystery, meant I never dared go inside. Looking around, the shop mainly sold leather underpants, underpants with straps instead of sides and underpants with bits of netting or gauze at the front, perhaps for swimming.

'Do you . . . do you have any ma–ma–magzz . . .? Magazines?'

The man didn't look up from the selection of butt plugs he was arranging on the counter next to a selection of witty greeting cards and bottles of poppers. 'Soft or hard, or d'you want, just, like, a magazine?'

'Oh, just, like, a magazine would be swell, thanks!' I smiled nervously.

'The main ones are over on the rack at the back, but let me know if you can't find anything you need,' he said, looking up with a wink. The whole place was actually very relaxed and the butt-plug guy was very friendly. Nonetheless, I was still terrified, my heart beating in my throat like I was on the threshold of some enormous adult rite of passage. I hurriedly bought a magazine called *OUT!* which, far from guys leaning back uncomfortably in their see-through underpants, turned out to contain some actually quite polite articles about new ways to wear coats and this summer's must-have chairs. In a way it was a lot like my mum's subscription to *Woman and Home*, except these articles were alongside listings for gay saunas, STI clinics and, inevitably, brunch spots.

Later that evening, back in my room at the hostel I put on my most shiny shoes, a shirt I'd bought in Marks and Spencer before I left and a pair of ill-fitting jeans, because that's what people seemed to wear in *Queer as Folk*, the Channel 4 series, which was my definitive point of reference for life as a gay man. It was set in Manchester and not New York but this felt immaterial and besides, both places had a lot of open brickwork. Too scared to get into a taxi after my last experience, I walked over to the West Village, the rain having given way to the last tinge of orange sunshine against the deep purple of the storm clouds, the concrete gleaming from its recent wash.

In *Queer as Folk*, the lead character, Nathan, goes into the first bar he sees and seems to immediately get chatting to loads of other people and then, emboldened by this, has the temerity to launch himself into the middle of the dance floor and then meets – and has sex – with the most handsome cool guy in the whole city. So it was clear that this was what I had to do – according to my only information, this was how the system worked.

On a street corner, I found a bar with another giant rainbow flag blowing in the wind and heard the sound of a piano player underscoring the chatter of confident, gregarious men inside in tight T-shirts and patterned vests. It could have been the gayest bar in all of Manhattan and maybe the whole world. I should have felt so relaxed and pleased to finally be somewhere like this at the start of this wonderful adventure, yet I didn't even have the courage to walk in.

Too scared, like the lion in the *Wizard of Oz*, I craned my neck to see through the windows as I scuttled past. Groups of friends catching up, drinking, laughing and joking together, waving cigarettes around as they spoke; I felt it would be impossible to go in on my own. Apart from anything else, I had no idea how I would talk to anyone unless they offered me a banana loaf.

I didn't stop walking until I reached Washington Square Park and stopped for a moment, realising I'd read it was a 'cruising ground', and it occurred to me that was something that gay men apparently did – hanging out in parks for sex.

Perhaps it had been a cruising ground in the 1920s but at this time, after a day of rain, it was completely empty, and suddenly I went from being terrified to being furious with myself. *Why haven't I got the guts to just live my life? Everyone else manages!* My mind raged at myself. *No one knows me here. I'm thousands of miles from home, so it should be perfect. Jeez, I can't even walk into a bar, never mind find the right place to have sex with a stranger in a bush!* Truth be told, if I had found someone to have sex with in a bush, I'd have been much too scared, and this circle of shame and frustration infuriated me. Also, I didn't have the right shoes on.

I took a deep breath and made myself walk back to the bar I'd left behind, determined that I had to make myself do this; I had to do something because I was an adult and I'd gone to all the trouble of coming to New York, thousands of miles away from the dessert trolley in Bromley. Pushing the glass door with its rainbow sticker above the handle, I stepped briskly past a wall covered in off-Broadway posters for Edith Piaf drag acts and cabaret shows with stars of the musicals.

Walking into the bar area, I tried to look confident by embodying what my dad had taught me; I stared straight ahead and looked like I might put up a fight if anyone tried to rob me. With my eyes fixed on the far side of the room, I began my march across, and in doing so, managed to walk straight into a low-level bar stool, which screeched into the table behind it, grazing my shin. People glanced up at the sheer awkwardness of it all, and I could feel my shoulders rising. It didn't matter – I ignored the pain, swallowed my yelp and kept going towards the bar with its open brickwork, mirrors and an actual framed photograph of Barry Manilow hanging proudly above the vodka bottles.

The piano player in the corner belted out a jazzy version of Alanis Morissette's 'Ironic', which did mean this was the gayest bar in the whole world, and the bartender cocked his world-weary ear towards me while he dried his cocktail shaker. I sputtered my order of a vodka tonic – with my slicked-back hair and a receding hairline no one checked my ID – while I awkwardly hoicked myself onto a high bar stool, trying to look cool but feeling as awkward as when I had to clamber out of the swimming pool at school.

Sat there, I sipped my drink as I criticised my reflection in the mirror and occasionally glanced at the men sat behind me at the small tables. Amongst the loud bursts of laughter and talking, I kept feeling self-conscious, as though everyone was looking at me, but at the same time frustrated that no one was looking at me. It was one thing to feel like an outsider around straight people, it was much worse to feel like an outsider when I was surrounded by my own tribe.

I had come a long way from pushing trifles up and down the golf-club dining room to sitting here in an actual gay bar in the middle of New York City, but I was just too embarrassed and self-conscious to speak to anyone, never mind make friends and meet some cool guy to have sex with in a bush, or even fall in love with. I just couldn't make that first step to strike up a chat, and it turns out if you look terrified and confused and keep rubbing your bruised leg, no one feels inclined to come and talk to you either.

The truth was, I didn't know what to expect from this adventure, but being so worked up, I knew I was in the wrong frame of mind to experience anything. Deflated and tired from the adrenaline rush, I was glad to finish my drink, grab my rain mac and slip out of there. I hurried back across the city, frustrated and annoyed at myself, the Empire State Building shining somewhere over me. I was sure there were exciting adventures to be had in this city, I just had no idea how to access them.

Back at the hostel, the Kiwi girl and her friend were sat in each other's arms in the lobby, but they didn't see me. I was relieved I hadn't been a third wheel on their date, though it dawned on me she'd probably invited me to join them because she'd felt sorry for me on my own in this big city. Exhausted from all the things that hadn't happened, I was only too glad to go to bed.

I had got out of Bromley, but somehow I couldn't escape it, even in New York. The following afternoon I got the Greyhound back to Providence, Rhode Island and I was delighted when Aunty Mary met me off the bus. We got a pizza on the way home.

8

Loving

Whenever I should be moving forward, I have a tendency to stay still or even go backwards. When I was twenty-one, I should have been getting ready to forge ahead with my life, but I didn't know how to. I still hadn't come out openly, and I was still living at home with my parents in Bromley. Having been involved with the National Youth Theatre – including dressing up as a rat in a touring schools production, amongst other things – when a call came from them, I was only too pleased to grab my briefcase, jump on the train and help out in their office on Holloway Road.

An extension of my love of errands, I loved being part of a team and having the routine of going to their office every day alongside the bustling commuters – it was almost like I was a normal person. I still felt like I was forty-six years old and still had a hard time having fun. As a teenager, I'd chosen to eschew the youthful round of making mistakes, getting drunk, taking drugs, falling in love, having your first kiss and getting fingered. Instead, I'd rejected all of this in favour of running mundane tasks with a series of suburban older women. I knew I had a lot of learning to catch up on.

I had never talked about my sexuality until one afternoon, while franking the mail, tired of being miserable keeping it bottled up, I casually mentioned that I really fancied this guy I'd seen on the train. Though it raised their eyebrows for a moment, my colleagues instinctively and brilliantly realised I didn't want to make a big deal talking about it, and without me having to say another thing, my best friend Alexa suggested we all go to the nightclub Heaven immediately, even though it was a Tuesday and the club wouldn't be open for at least another three hours. When we got inside, my friends, who were all girls, put their handbags in the middle of the empty dance floor (empty because it was the middle of the week and we were the first through the door) and danced round them in the darkness and dry ice until we had to leave to get our last trains home.

While this didn't change things directly, it felt like the shackles of my Victorian closet – an *armoire*, if you will – were starting to come off, and I was seeing my life in new ways. I was like Dorothy stepping out of that windswept house to find the world in glorious Technicolor – but rather than a house, I was stepping out of Holloway Road Tube station and in place of upbeat munchkins and representatives of the Lollipop Guild, I encountered a man with no trousers and an old lady shouting at a bin. It didn't matter that it was less enchanting – it was life and I was alive to it.

Even the incidental seemed to burst to life – our regular sandwich shop seemed like the set of a prison drama. 'Tell Penny she's a bitch and that's from Lola!' I was told on collecting a jacket potato, which led me to fantasise that the whole team were on day release from nearby Holloway Prison, their crimes unknown aside from burnt potatoes and whatever it was Penny had done.

Errands I had to run on behalf of the finance manager made me feel like a spy. I was told to take a carrier bag and 'try to not look like you're carrying two grand in one-pound coins, and when you get to the bank, ask for Joan – she's expecting you'. It all seemed so glamorous, but after a misdemeanour with the finance manager over some misplaced panpipes, I was no longer entrusted with bags of cash any more.

My dreams of being a performer in some way had been sublimated into franking the post and changing the water cooler, but I still loved Alan Bennett, Noël Coward and Victoria Wood. They were all able to reflect the subtle nuances of the world back in such a way that elevated the everyday.

However, I couldn't see how *I* would go about doing what my heroes did. For example, the comedians I'd seen on television at this time seemed to be straight, white men with confident views of themselves and the world – they didn't waste time with insecurities, holding up towels to hide themselves in the changing rooms. They seemed supremely assured in themselves, and what they had to say. I'd never been to a comedy club because they seemed like dark basement bars with people smoking, drinking and shouting out violent heckles at will, which couldn't have been further from my delicate Noël Coward sensibilities.

So, it seemed like a bizarre dare when a few friends of mine from the National Youth Theatre suggested that I should try stand-up. Sam Battersea and her husband Charlie Baker put it to me one day when I was franking the mail again, but now much more flamboyantly. Sam had been doing sketches in Edinburgh for years while Charlie had just tried doing his first few gigs and thought I should give it a go too. They assured me that being the least likely person to turn up to do stand-up would be part of the charm, and I liked the idea of pulling off such an outrageous stunt. That's all it felt like at this point, a stunt, not unlike doing a Julie Walters monologue in a school cabaret, just to show the world that I liked being unusual.

I sought advice from everywhere I could and was, as you can imagine, very happy to be guided by Sam and Charlie, Charlie Hayes, Keith Palmer, Ria Parry, Paul Roseby and John Hoggarth. Always seeking to be obtuse, rather than looking to the wealth of comics out there for inspiration, I, instead, started listening to Rufus Wainwright. For the first time, I heard someone sing about things that weren't just love, they were songs about phones on vibrate and men reading fashion magazines – more of the ephemeral things I liked to notice too.

My first gig was at Bethnal Green Working Men's Club. It wasn't quite as blokey as the club's name suggests as this was the boom of the East End hipster scene and it was actually a charity fundraiser with performances from musicians, burlesque acts and sketch comedians with an audience of trendy media types, who were actually much more terrifying than a traditional blokey working-men's-club crowd.

I got the bus there after work and listened to the Scissor Sisters on my CD Walkman. I really wanted to stay on the bus and go somewhere – anywhere – else. I couldn't understand why I was putting myself through this ordeal and, in some way, felt like it was another set of hoops to jump through to feel OK about being me. I was, for once, early, so I said to myself, *Just go near the venue and see how you feel*. Which I did, felt terrible, and then went for a walk round the block to see if I felt any better.

Eventually, I saw that the lights were on inside the club and decided that it was now or never and walked in while trying to look not-terrified. It's weird that we live in a world where we have to hide everything we genuinely feel – I should have walked in and gone, 'Hi, I'm Tom and I'm doing my first ever stand-up set at the event tonight, and I'm absolutely terrified and I want to run away!'

The trouble is, people often don't know how to respond to this sort of honesty. It's somehow seen as an imposition to ask someone else to empathise, so we put on a performance to make strangers feel OK. There's a fear everyone might start being emotionally honest all the time and the streets would be full of people shouting their innermost feelings at one another – 'Please help me! I'm worried about doing my tax return and that one day I'm going to die!' – which might really hamper people trying to get on their bus.

'I'm Tom and I'm here to do the gig,' I said to the big-chested security guard who didn't look at me.

'What?' he grunted back. He couldn't hear me because I was speaking inaudibly.

'I'm here to do the gig tonight! I'm Tom!' I said bravely, but still terrified that he might question what exactly I was 'doing' at the gig. Maybe he'd tell me I didn't look very funny, and I'd agree. He didn't though; he just stood aside and opened the door, still looking off into the distance like I wasn't there. I wandered into the fake-wood-panelled room where the sound guy was setting up busily. His T-shirted, lanky frame looked up.

'Hi, I'm Tom, I'm here to do the gig?'

'To do what?'

'I . . .' The saliva dried up in my throat. 'I'm here to do the gig . . . tonight?'

'Oh, right. You're early.'

I'd assumed this would be a good thing, but his face didn't suggest that he was pleased. He said I may as well do a 'sound check', which involved speaking into the microphone. Since I'd never done this before and, in fact, never held a microphone, it felt mortifying, especially as I hated the sound of my own voice. The sound guy seemed even more irritated that I didn't know what to do with a microphone. I was reluctant to hold it near me for fear that it would make my horrible voice even louder. 'You've got to hold it up to your mouth. It won't work otherwise,' he shouted from the darkness at the back of the room.

I can't really remember much about the gig itself other than I'd invited my friend Dean to come along and support me. Dean has the biggest heart and while being a bear of a man is also capable of doing back flips, which, if you saw him, would surprise you. He was perfect at being my only friend in the room because he intuitively knew what I needed, which was largely just to stand near me against the radiator at the back and when I looked up at him, he'd say, 'You all right? You got this.'

When my name was called, I bounced onto the stage and started talking – I knew I just had to keep going until the end. The sooner it was over, the sooner I could be back on that bus listening to the Scissor Sisters. With the guidance of friends, I'd prepared a story about going to watch my first football game – the Millwall game I'd been taken to by my colleagues at the golf club. It didn't have any jokes in it, it was just a story about me not fitting in, really, but I thought there was something funny about it.

I gabbled through most of it until at one point I was on a tangent talking about how my mum worked on first-floor fashions at The Army & Navy, and one of the trendy types shouted out, 'Well, that doesn't sound like fashion!' and people around her laughed. Without thinking about it I just shouted back, 'Like you would know!' and suddenly people laughed and clapped. It wasn't a clever thing to say, but somewhere in my soul I knew I had to say something – I suppose it was the first time I'd stood up for myself. In moments like that, audiences like people to stand up for themselves because it means they don't have to worry about you and maybe gives them hope that they might be able to stand up for themselves too.

Before I knew it, the gig was done and I was at the back of the room again with Dean, who gave me a thumbs up in the darkness. We couldn't talk as the next act was on stage doing something with a hula hoop. We walked to Bethnal Green Tube station before we went our separate ways – him to his flat in Muswell Hill and me back to Bromley. 'I'm really proud of you, mate,' he said, giving me a bear hug. I didn't think anything – I was just glad it was done. I'd completed the dare.

As a result of making this start, I was encouraged by my friends to enter a competition for new comedians called So You Think You're Funny?, which involved travelling all the way to the Edinburgh Fringe on my own to perform a set. I got through to the semi-finals. A lot of people love going to the festival because it feels like a huge celebration of performing arts. However, I was totally overwhelmed by it and went in the opposite direction to the throngs of people and spent my time at the world's largest arts festival hiding in Marks and Spencer, trying to calm down.

I managed somehow to get through the semi-finals and ended up being in the finals, which meant performing in front of four hundred people, and somehow I won the whole thing. It was a really lovely feeling – a relief even – that made me smile very broadly to realise that people enjoyed my set and they connected with what I was talking about.

I also made some wonderful friends there, including Sarah Millican, Kevin Bridges, Stuart Goldsmith, Emma Fryer and Joe Wilkinson, and I feel lucky to have started out at the same time as people who are generous and kind and who I'm still able to lean on now.

Off the back of this competition, I was encouraged to do another one – the BBC New Comedy Awards, which I also won. I was amazed. I think it was just that I seemed an unlikely type of person to become a stand-up and I think the judges applauded my audacity really.

The day after the awards, in typically peculiar fashion, I continued the celebrations by going for an STI test – a response to my inability to enjoy anything for too long. Being celebrated on stage with these competitions, I knew that surely some sort of punishment was nearing and this would no doubt be how I'd get my comeuppance.

I went for the full range of tests including one for HIV and managed to get myself worked up about the whole experience. It is difficult to explain to anyone unaware how HIV/AIDS hangs over many gay people, even now. As a child in the 1990s, I knew that men like Freddie Mercury were dying from the disease, but watching the news, I wasn't able to ask questions which made it feel all the more terrifying. I can only imagine how terrifying it must have been for those directly effected. Nowadays, HIV is a very manageable condition. Even in the mid-noughties, treatments meant that many people with HIV would live long, healthy lives, yet still the fear and anguish pervaded.

My sexual antics had been largely limited to one incident involving a futon and another experience in Cirencester with a Liberal Democrat. However, when the needle was produced to take the blood from my arm, I abruptly passed out and had to be brought back to consciousness by the nurse, who was waving smelling salts under my nose as though I was a Victorian lady – in so many ways it was proving impossible to hide who I truly was. The test came back negative.

So my career seemed to be moving forward, and I was even starting to feel better about myself – maybe this was the time I'd finally get to experience love. What that actually meant, I still wasn't sure, beyond what I'd seen in musicals. A friend of mine at work set me up with her friend Daniel, who apparently had seen me at a party and quite liked me. Normally, I would have thought anyone who liked me had some very poor judgement issues and should be ignored (plus, I already had a well-established type – straight men who could never be interested in me), but I thought I should give Daniel a chance, seeing as my friend said he was a nice guy and we were about the same height.

Daniel was invited to one of our Friday pizza nights after work, which usually involved drinking cheap white wine and then heading to the local pizza restaurant where they served sticks of bread in a glass as soon as you sat down, which to my mind was highly sophisticated and very continental. This was also a time when we were proudly European and I had even made myself start drinking the ultimate Italian apéritif, Campari and soda, which, while looking bright-pink and fun, tasted to me like hairspray.

Daniel arrived and I initially couldn't work out why anyone would think us compatible. However, after a long time chatting, we realised we both liked Victoria Wood's *Dinnerladies*, and Daniel rubbed his leg against mine under the table. Like a dog. I'd never experienced confidence like it, and I was immediately in love. We spent the night where he was house-sitting in Kentish Town for his aunt, who was away even though her cat was dying.

This was also the first time I'd had any kind of sexual encounter where I wasn't drunk, and Daniel was much more confident than me – he had a nose piercing. Also, he'd had a boyfriend. Although he'd been dumped by him, so I guess we both felt vulnerable one way or another. In the morning, I didn't hate myself, which was also a first, and we even went out for a walk along the Southbank. I remember thinking to myself, *This is what it feels like to be like everybody else!*

We spent most evenings together that week, and on one of them, he'd bought a new coat. I noticed it because it was the same as mine. Maybe he liked me. He was due to go back to university in Leeds that weekend, where he was studying chemistry. Unlike me, he wasn't worried about his parents dying as soon as he left the house. In fact, he was barely worried about the dying cat downstairs.

On the Thursday, he said he had a sore throat, so he wasn't sure if we should meet up. I immediately went to the supermarket and bought him soup (chicken soup like Aunty Jilly had made for me once when I was ill), paracetamol, cough lozenges, cough syrup and tissues. I dropped it round to the house in Kentish Town. He answered the door in his pyjamas (funny place to have a door) and despite looking confused that I was there, said thank you.

On the way home he texted to say, 'Thanks for the soup!' and I felt exultant. It's hard to convey just how important a single text message was at the time. Before the limitless messaging of today, a text message was like a letter, something typed thoughtfully from one person to another with consideration and succinct clarity to fit within the 160-character limit of all text messages. The number of messages you could send was dictated by your phone tariff – the number of messages you could keep was limited by the storage on your phone (for a generation largely frozen out of getting a mortgage, phone contracts were the first time we had been introduced to the idea of credit, payment plans and the obligations of contracts).

In my gay abandon – again, quite literally – I hadn't realised that my overexcited chicken soup buying might have seemed suffocating to Daniel. The following night I asked him how he thought it would work going forward. 'How would what work?' he asked flippantly, with his head on my shoulder.

'Us!' I said, surprised, though trying not to raise voices, especially since he had a sore throat.

'How could "us" work? We'll be too far away.'

I thought to myself that yet again this wasn't what happened in movies and in musicals – you don't finally meet the one and then they get obsessed with geography. And anyway he was supposed to be studying chemistry. I let the conversation change before bringing up the subject again. 'You don't think we could visit and stuff?'

'Well, you could if you liked? But it wouldn't be the same – too far away.'

'But . . . don't you think it's worth it?'

'To be honest, Tom, this was really just a bit of fun for me.'

I somehow managed to hear this as 'This has been so much fun for me. Please come to visit me, at university, in Leeds.' His delighted surprise seemed somewhat muted when I texted him the following week to tell him I'd booked a ticket and would be coming up that weekend. That Saturday, I duly jumped on a train but thought it would make me look more casual

– bohemian even – if I packed my overnight things in two paper carrier bags. The effect was missed and, catching sight of myself in the reflection of the train window, I realised it made me look like the pigeon woman in *Home Alone 2*.

When I arrived, he wasn't at the station. I waited and then used up one of my texts to tell him 'I'm here!' He apologised profusely and said he'd misunderstood what train I was on. Twenty minutes later, he dutifully arrived to meet me, drunk – though I didn't mind. The poor guy had been too nice to outright dump me – or perhaps such a brief fling hadn't warranted the conversation – and now I'd foolishly turned up in the middle of his hedonistic university weekend.

He took me out to meet his friends, who smoked like confident characters in a Noël Coward play, which I resented because surely looking down at people was *my* special thing. They looked at me snootily when Daniel introduced me. 'This is Tom,' he said, gesturing to the 'bit-of-fun' bag lady who'd just trekked all the way from London. The next day he took me out for breakfast before I got the train back to London and then across London back to Bromley. He didn't say he didn't want to see me again, but I knew it.

'How's things with you and Daniel?!' our mutual friend asked gleefully, but I couldn't tell her the humiliating truth. I thought I had handled it well until I was told he was seeing someone else – someone cool from uni, no doubt. What was perhaps more alarming was despite feeling heartbroken for the first time in my life, I now had to go on stage and try to make other people happy, because after the competitions I was now getting booked for gigs as a stand-up comedian.

Trying to talk to friends about this new heartbreak sensation I'd be met with, 'I guess it was only a bit of fun though, right?'

not realising that 'fun' was not something I'd ever signed up for – I wasn't good at sport and I didn't like board games because they made a mess. 'Fun' seemed like the opposite of what I was experiencing. More than this, it didn't feel like I could brush it off as just another fling because I'd waited my whole life to find anyone to make a connection with, so it didn't feel like they came along too often. In terms of numbers, perhaps for straight people especially, it seems there are just more people to have those fun flings with. For me, it felt like I'd been stranded on a desert island for years and the one time a plane had gone overhead, I'd failed to wave it down.

Now the mid-noughties and online dating was just starting to emerge, which should have helped me find another plane to hail – a great many people had taken to using early models including Gaydar, which had lists of men with details of their hobbies and penis size (and for many of them, penis size *was* their hobby). Older or more confident friends of mine had taken to the site as early adopters and met life partners and friends but, typically, I'd felt it was something reserved solely for other people and by the time I eventually plucked up the courage to sign up, it had evolved into something different. An efficient – at times, aggressive – means by which to meet up for sex, with a whole host of men predisposed to disdain anyone for 'wasting their time' by not knowing 'what they want'. It was very intimidating for anyone, especially someone who occasionally wore a cravat. A brief online discussion around 'What are you into?' was not, I quickly came to realise, an invitation to discuss one's interests in gardening and the latter films of Ingmar Bergman.

While it is easy for me to be cynical, the power of online dating sites and latterly apps like Grindr shouldn't be underestimated in terms of their impact on the queer community. For the first time, it was possible to know that you weren't the only gay person in your area; no longer did you have to feel so isolated; and for once you didn't have to trek to some far-off geographic location to try to meet people.

I tried to make it work for me, but while I made some wonderful long-term friends and had long chats with people I never saw again, my notable experiences included meeting up with a guy who brought a Scrabble set with him and another who spent our date looking at the app trying to find someone else to meet him. One guy just needed to talk. He told me that his partner had died the previous year, and then he said, 'I still leave him voicemails, to tell him how I'm doing, what's been happening with me – is that weird?' If nothing else, I've come to learn that nothing's really weird. I think we're all just trying to get through the day – and the night – sometimes it's simply connections we need; to feel like we're worth spending time with, even if it's just for a short time.

Feeling down about my own unusual heartbreak, I thought there might be something wrong with me, shamed at not grasping the reality of the situation as a 'bit of fun' – but then I realised that all songs, poems, plays, art and films are about the foibles of how people fall in and out of love. So now I was both heartbroken and furious that I wasn't even original.

I went from feeling like I had always been a middle-aged man to suddenly feeling like I was twelve years old, and yet again I was in the wrong place at the wrong age. I wasn't in school where you can make mistakes and everyone expects you to fall in love and get your heartbroken – I was in an office doing admin and trying to be a stand-up comedian and I had the anguish of paying off my phone contract.

On the back of winning two newcomer competitions, people started thinking that I was the new act they'd want to book for their comedy club, but what they got instead was a sad twenty-two-year-old who had somehow found himself delivering whimsical stories about golf-club dessert trollies to braying stag parties who were apoplectic with rage – incandescent at how different I was to them. It was like singing Judy Garland's 'Get Happy' while crying hysterically. I was a mess.

It seems odd to me that schools don't teach you how to deal with feeling sad; they teach you trigonometry and how to measure a corner using algebra, but seldom how to get yourself out of one. If I had an idea for a routine, I couldn't imagine how to make it funny. I simply didn't have the mental energy; I couldn't think clearly at all – the gears had jammed. Nothing was funny or light to me – I was driving with the handbrake on again.

I think not having any guidance on how to deal with these feelings and still feeling too ashamed to talk about them meant that the sadness became even more entrenched. The petulant child within who'd dared to do an Alan Bennett monologue in Year 9 and even had the audacity to perform stand-up to hipsters was now adamant he would not let this sad episode pass without acknowledgement.

I did a gig in Birmingham where halfway through the set someone shouted out, 'You fucking poof!' and everybody laughed. He seemed to know what the audience wanted much more than I did, and realising there was no way back, I panicked and left the stage. I didn't have the life skills or the stage experience to know how to deal with this heckle (other than shouting back, 'Yes, I suppose that's true!'). The booker phoned me the following day to say sorry about the bad gig; it sounded tough 'But because you left the stage early, we can only pay you half the money.'

Although I didn't tell him what had been said, Dad advised me, 'You've got to learn some put-downs when they shout things out.' He was trying his best to help, still arming me like he had against the threat of muggers. It was just that I knew it wasn't about having clever lines to throw out at the audience, it was much more about being happy with myself because otherwise audiences could see my vulnerability and they didn't like it – it reminded them of their own.

People wanted to book me, but when I got on stage, most of the time I just couldn't deliver the gig. Other people seemed to be able to do it just fine, but then that's often how life seems – we torture ourselves that other people are coping, compounding the sense there's something wrong with us for not being fallible. In my mind, Daniel was having a confident, grown-up relationship accompanied by grown-up profound feelings – not the beginners class he'd had with me, awkward and inexperienced with an occasional 'Ow!' when an arm got trapped.

Up until now, I didn't drink very much alcohol, mainly as I was anxious about becoming like the teenagers in my year at school who got out of control and embarrassed themselves. But now, I was frustrated at how I hadn't used that time to experiment; maybe I wouldn't be in this situation now if I'd learnt about myself at the appropriate time. So alcohol now represented getting out of control and experimentation, but also escape, a way of switching off the voice in my head beating me up and dragging my mood down all the time – in my mind, it was a way to just be free.

I had no idea of my limits when having a few drinks at a party – I once passed out on an exercise bike, at another I was midway through the Macarena – out of nowhere, I'd be flung through time and space and abruptly wake up on a sofa or a makeshift bed. Confused and frightened about where I was and how I'd got there, it would slowly dawn on me as the room re-orientated and I realised I was at a friend's house, just looking at it from the unfamiliar angle of the floor.

These undignified moments made me realise I had to make a change. Rather than running away any further, I knew I needed to confront something, and someone, with the truth. For someone who felt like they were born in the wrong era, I thought I'd never actually come out – after all, Victorian gentlemen don't need to tell anyone about their sexuality. I'd taken Mum to a Rufus Wainwright concert and then made us walk to Charing Cross to get the train home, even though we could have got the Tube.

'Why don't we just get the Underground?'

'Oh, it's quicker,' I said sheepishly. There was no way I was going to have what seemed like a massive conversation with my mum on a crowded yet silent Tube coming back from Shepherd's Bush Empire. I thought to myself, *Just get through this*.

The landscape has changed significantly since the mid-2000s. I feel if I came out on a quiet Tube train now, someone would film it on their phone, people in the train carriage would clap and applaud and hug and cry and it would be a great thing for that random person to put on their social media to get five million 'likes'. By contrast, in the mid-2000s, people would have just looked embarrassed, annoyed even, that someone had interrupted the silence.

When I finally told my mum that evening, walking through the Friday-night crowds, she said she'd always known. It was as if those forays into dressing up, singing Noël Coward songs and obsessing about place settings had given me away. In the spirit of protecting the family, Mum gave me the advice to not tell my dad yet. He was born in 1941 – it was a different time – and no one likes a row. It's best if we just wait to work out the best way to tell him.

'Do you think I should move out then?' I asked as we walked down the Charing Cross Road, past the Astoria, Gina G blasting out of the nightclub G-A-Y. I thought this would give Mum some context, but in truth it terrified her more as Gina G did seem very loud.

'No, no, don't move out – that's not what I mean darling, I don't want you to feel like you have to run away'. I realise now she was just trying to protect us from each other. We got home and talked late into the night.

I was still learning how to be myself on stage more and more. The burn from Daniel was still there – I tried dating other people, but it wasn't the same and I was terrified that going through heartbreak again would just make going on stage as a comedian ever more difficult.

I'm lucky. Mum and Dad have always been supportive of me on stage and been there for good gigs and bad gigs, always with the same smiling faces, even when I'm up there making fun of their eccentricities to rooms full of strangers. They're on stage with me even when they're not in the room.

I never talked about being gay in my gigs before I was out, though frankly I doubt anyone would be surprised, and in my mind, I was sure no one would want to hear about it anyway. I also saw myself as having hardly any experience of it – except for all the napkin folding – so it was hardly something I could talk about with any authority.

At a gig in a converted public toilet in Shepherds Bush, Mum and Dad were there to see me come off stage triumphantly after doing another of my camp story skits to an audience who seemed to get my sense of humour. The compère came on afterwards and in a sarcastic voice said, 'That was Tom Allen and I think he might be gay . . .' to which everyone laughed all over again, but in a different way. I realised they'd been laughing at me and not with me. Mum knew but Dad didn't, so I couldn't even mention it.

I decided enough was enough of hiding and living in fear of what a comedy club compère might say next. I phoned Dad one day when I was working on a Saturday – someone had to be there to open the car park barrier. I was alone in the office. A phone call worked for me as it meant we could hang up afterwards. Dad was upset – more so because he knew I must have kept this a secret for so long. He talked about George Michael being on *Parkinson* and how him talking upfront about it meant it broke down barriers. Dad must've known all along and was just waiting patiently for me to tell him. In the meantime, he'd tried to educate himself as best he could, looking for clues and references.

It wasn't as if everything was now finally sorted out and I then had the strength to go and have a series of perfect relationships and buy a flat with hanging baskets. If anything, it marked just the beginning of getting things out in the open. I think somehow it taught me that comedy isn't about pushing your sad feelings down; it's about acknowledging them and still finding a way to be funny. And when I realised that, I started to really love it.

9

Cruising

I once went cruising. It was on a boat. It wasn't in the woods or in the back of a car park, as I understand some gay cruising is. I was booked to perform on a gay cruise out of the blue – quite literally. The booking came in from a company I didn't know, and I wasn't sure how they'd heard of me, but I was very glad to do a gig that didn't involve getting a train across the country all day and a sandwich at a Whistlestop station café. Also, I really needed the money.

I was in a steady routine of travelling around various comedy clubs, and while I could say I was scraping a living, I was still terrified of being rejected by audiences if they didn't get what I meant and end up feeling even more alone about how I saw the world. I stuck to my material – too afraid to write anything new because I was convinced what I was saying was the only version of myself audiences would be able to get on board with. It felt at times like I was apologising for being me, or at least explaining who I was.

Financially, I didn't have the security to take any risks and felt like I had to do any gig offered to me just to keep money coming in – to pay my bills and to prove that I could make a living from such a precarious occupation. It wasn't such a bad policy because it did mean I was getting stage experience everywhere, and I was also meeting and watching lots of other acts who were great to learn from. Since I usually travelled alone and stood on stage on my own, it was nice to talk to people to see if they were going through the same rollercoaster of emotions as I was, the ups and downs of good gigs and bad gigs.

Still unable to drive, I'd end up stuck in places after a gig, staying in whatever accommodation was within my limited price range. It was the early days of using maps on my phone, and trying to find my hotel, it took me round a town twice before leading me to the front door of the local hospital. Twice.

Eventually I found a sign for the B&B I'd booked – a dark gravel driveway led off the main road at the sign for Frog House. Approaching the huge Victorian door, I pressed the doorbell. A light came on inside the building, and I could hear someone shuffling around. Then the door was wrenched open to reveal the B&B owner, who looked entirely like a frog.

She was wearing shimmering metallic leggings and a close-fitting green top and big square glasses to magnify her eyes. She was at least eighty-five years old. 'You must be Tom!' she said in a voice that sounded posh and also frightening. With a kick of her leg to the side and a gesture of her hand, she beckoned me in before immediately lifting her hand to remove strands of wild hair out of her face.

The overhead light lit the entrance hall but in the darkness of the corridors leading off it, I could see the entire building was themed around frogs – pictures of frogs on the walls, a small ceramic frog sat on the check-in desk and even the walls were themed around frogs, in that they were green. 'I just love frogs!' she said, unnecessarily, again gesturing wildly and sticking out one leg.

I have a mild fear of slimy things that jump and despite having grown up watching *The Muppet Show,* I'd not associate frogs with any kind of hospitality because intrinsically they seem cold and slimy. 'This is your room and the bathroom is just back through there.' She gestured to the other end of the hallway. 'Down the steps, put on the light, and it's the second door on the left.'

'Oh, thank you,' I said politely.

'When you're through the door, there's a staircase. Take that down two flights to the basement. There's two doors, which are cupboards, and then next to them, on the left, is the door to the bathroom. Do be careful not to make too much noise as my husband is a very light sleeper.' I realised I should perhaps have plumped for an ensuite.

Opening the door to my room, I was surprised to see that it wasn't green, but instead, bright orange. The bedspread was green, though – a sort of shimmering green that matched the landlady's leggings. I couldn't see myself relaxing here, never mind dragging myself through the creepy frog-themed house in the middle of the night to use the bathroom. In the corner of my bedroom was a sink, which I imagined had found other uses by previous guests also too scared to walk to the bathroom. Next to the sink was a bin, naturally shaped like a frog. Next to the frog bin was a bottle of Febreze, and I think it was this that sealed the deal for me; a product famous for masking odours – treating the symptom, but not the cause – I decided to leave. I spent my entire fee for the gig staying in a Travelodge – corporate, sterile and utterly perfect.

When the email arrived offering me a series of gigs with accommodation included (because they were onboard a cruise ship), I knew it was a gig that might take me places. Quite literally. And it certainly wouldn't involve frogs.

It was a cruise ship chartered by an American company that specialised in putting American gays on boats and sailing them off for their 'vacation'. This one was starting in northern Italy and taking in the various islands and coastal towns of the Mediterranean. I had no idea what to expect other than I was to fly to Venice to board the ship, which would take me round various ports during which time I was to perform as part of a live showcase and then deliver two longer sets later in the week. Apart from that, I was free to enjoy the cruise.

I was in my late twenties by this point, but due to my hang-ups, still struggled to wholeheartedly enjoy pretty much anything from birthday parties to nights out to trips abroad. On this occasion, it wasn't a totally unmerited sense of trepidation either – I didn't know anyone on the boat, I didn't know if the American audience would get my humour and if I didn't like it, I had no idea how I would get off this gigantic vessel.

Nevertheless, I applied my tried and trusted method of trying not to think about it and flew to Venice and then, as instructed in my confirmation email, boarded a taxi boat to the port. That's where the instructions ended, and I was very worried that once at the harbour, I'd be unable to find the boat and then I was clueless as to what to do next.

When I got there, it was apparent that working out where the gay cruise was leaving from was indeed very straightforward. Mainly because, if you've never seen a cruise ship before, it's essentially a multi-storey car park with balconies that sits in a port like a block of flats with a funnel that turns up on skylines pretty much out of nowhere.

Secondly, literally thousands of gay men in brightly coloured vests, wearing sunglasses on their heads or on the ends of their noses, were marching their wheelie cases in one direction. This they did with the casual confidence that comes from years of perching an expensive holdall on your wrist and trying to move quickly while wearing Prada sandals. This they did with ease while shouting to their friends, who were all in other groups of gay men waving their sunglasses high above their heads back at them.

They shouted to one another in the way that people who like each other enough can be horrible without taking offence: 'Er, honey, where are you going? The clap clinic is back thataway!'

'Fuck you!' they shouted back, laughing. They used 'she' to refer to one another, which is part of centuries-old gender play – or maybe it's just a way of owning the bullying we'd all no doubt suffered.

'Most people go on vacation to put their feet up – she only goes to put her feet down!' they screeched about another member of their group followed by more laughing as they delighted in being reunited for this celebratory time.

I have always been a snob predicated on not really liking other people, especially anyone who reminds me of myself, and until this time I had held a deep-seated notion that a cruise would be something I'd hate. To my mind, it would be full of gluttonous people who loved buffets and who couldn't be bothered to travel the world under their own steam so needed a huge tower block to deliver them to the periphery of a city just so they could say they'd been there. However, this time it was different. Maybe it was the immaculate running of the ship by the thousands of staff, or maybe it was that this many gays having fun was irresistible – just look at Eurovision.

I left my bag at the allocated place, basically a lectern in a car park in front of the ship, and the man smiled at me so I trusted him – I had ten dollars in my pocket, the rest in my sock and I was taking my organs with me, so the risk was minimal. I then ascended the gangplank to the entrance of this ocean liner. It was everything I dreaded – people who looked confidently happy with their lives and an interior design that involved swirly carpets and brassy fittings. The cruise director, a tall American man, introduced himself with the question. 'Hug?'

I tentatively said, 'Sure,' since no one had ever presented themselves to me like that and certainly never in Bromley.

He hugged me like an old friend and surreptitiously spun me round so that before I knew it I was in the middle of the swirly carpet and he was on to the next polo-shirt-with-a-popped-collar-wearing passenger boarding. 'Oh hello, dear – this isn't a clap clinic, you know!' more raucous laughter.

'Champagne?' a handsome waiter appeared at my elbow out of nowhere with a tray and I immediately went from snobbish disdain to loving it. My first experience of this cruise had been mainly simple questions: 'Hug?', 'Champagne?' and I wondered if there were really any other questions in the whole world.

I found my room – or 'cabin' – to be compact but perfectly formed, complete with a gift on the bed of a sports holdall from the cruise company to use on future trips to help me easily spot other gays headed to the ship. Then, just as I was settling in, the man who had hugged me aboard was on the tannoy. 'Ahh, hello!' I'd never heard anyone quite as bright and full of hope. I could hear people in neighbouring cabins calling hello back like we were in a gay American version of *Hi-de-Hi!* 'Please make your way to the main theatre for our cruise welcome speech!'

As soon as I opened my cabin door, everyone was quietly weaving through the corridors to the main auditorium. Suddenly, it was like being at school again but this time a fabulous school – gay school – during a fire drill, with everyone filing in the same direction smiling excitedly in their bright vest tops and rugby shorts and not dreading lining up in the car park.

At my real, much less fabulous, school, the fire bell seemed to be going off endlessly – set off by unruly Year 8s who'd forgotten their food-tech ingredients and were desperate for a way out. Arriving at the staff car park to line up in our form groups, there'd always be one sorry class of girls who'd been in the swimming pool on hearing the alarm and been made to go outside (even though they'd protested that being in water would surely save them from fire) and huddled freezing in their towels and swimming caps at one side of the tennis courts. The gay boys in their class would be delighted to be reunited with their friends and not made to continue running around the field playing rugby or football with the other boys who they'd basically never spoken to before.

This fantastic gay assembly involved the upbeat cruise director telling us how the cruise would work – basically it was going to be wall to wall *fun*! Everyone applauded, because that's how Americans respond to things. We then gave a round of applause for all the different nationalities who were there – the largest group definitely being American – for which there was more applause. A special standing ovation was given for the group who'd bravely made their way from the less than gay-friendly Russia. Everyone wiped away a tear.

We were then told in no uncertain terms that we were to make friends with everybody. As the cruise director said, 'When you're out and about on the ship, keep your head up, say hello to people and smile – ask them how their day is going. Don't keep staring at your phone – you do not need a dating app to tell you that the man next to you is *still gay!*' Everyone tittered and put their phone down, embarrassed at being caught.

'. . . Also, there isn't a country anywhere in the world where it is *legal* to have sex on your balcony, so please don't do that at any point.' A number of crestfallen faces nodded in disappointed agreement.

The result of the cruise director's instruction was that all the confident Americans chatted to everyone. I'd always dreamed of living in a world where people said hello to each other – like Belle walking down the street in *Beauty and the Beast*. Where I had grown up, even straight people avoided being too outgoing, or even nice to one another, for fear that it might look flamboyant or worse, weak.

In Bromley, people's biggest fear was being 'mugged off' or being 'taken for a mug'. This isn't an identity issue to do with large-handled tea cups, but more to do with being naïve or being made a fool of. It's quite a broad spectrum though, and to be 'mugged off' includes being overcharged by a builder for your loft conversion, getting overtaken on the dual carriageway and stretches all the way to being outright murdered.

Onboard this gay monolith of a cruise ship, people were encouraged to behave in a way that was the opposite of this. Which seemed ironic because historically, as a people, we've been prone to being mugged off in all its forms. The huge engines started with a massive judder and we were off on our voyage, the tower block now growling its way through the grand canal of Venice, dwarfing the idyllic rivers running between the mediaeval squares and palazzos. The floor beneath me shook and didn't stop the entirety of the trip.

The outward confidence of my shipmates was in abundance everywhere. Cabin doors were decorated in ribbons and pompoms – just like the ones I'd tried to put round my mirror as a teenager – and there were whiteboards for leaving messages for the inhabitants and sashes garlanded the door frames with proud slogans such as *Liberté, Egalité . . . Beyoncé!*

Still getting my bearings among all the swirly carpets and the brassy handrails, I decided I had to experience the formal dining room. I was informed that, terrifyingly, they don't have tables for solo diners and that you had to share.

I entered underneath a huge chandelier – a monstrous sculpture of glass and more brass, like a giant drag queen's earring. Having been told to sit anywhere I could find a space, I could feel my shoulders hunching nervously – it was like being at school all over again, trying to find somewhere to sit in the canteen. The shakings of the ship had turned to broad sways as we sailed onward into the wide-open sea, which meant it was often hard to keep my balance. People must have thought I was drunk – at one point, I grabbed a tray of bread rolls for stability.

Trying to embody my dad's advice, I still walked everywhere as though I had a purpose and kept a stern face like I'd put up a fight if anyone approached me. This probably just made me look even more drunk as I faltered in standing upright. After circling the groups of people already sat together chatting, I was starting to run out of steam and contemplated just running back to my cabin or maybe getting in one of the lifeboats and rowing back to England.

A handsome man in his fifties rose from his table with courtly politeness – something I've found to be a virtue among so many Americans – and standing in my path asked. 'Do you like vaginas?'

It would be an odd question in any circumstance, but was especially so in the context of this ship. I didn't want to appear rude, but I feared it was a crass question about my sexuality or worse, perhaps he was somehow mocking me like the bullies at school who'd ask a trick question like, 'If-you're-gay-say-what,' and you'd respond, 'What?' and they'd laugh in your face.

I firmly said, 'No.'

The man looked crestfallen and also mildly affronted. I wasn't sure what he expected me to say. He turned to leave and I took it upon myself to pursue the matter. 'Why do you ask?'

'Well, you looked like you were on your own.'

I was confused. 'Sorry, did you ask me if I liked vaginas?'

'No.' he looked even more affronted, because Americans can be quite formal at times. 'I said, "Would you like to join us?"'

'Oh! I thought you were asking me if I liked vaginas!' He looked confused and still a little affronted. 'I'd be delighted,' I said, pulling out a chair before the polite man could change his mind. Suddenly remembering the mandate from the gay assembly earlier, I did as I was told. 'Hello, I'm Tom. It's nice to meet you all!'

Despite my initial trepidation, it actually felt nice to be sat with this gathering of strangers; I suddenly realised we were *all* strangers, not just me, none of us really knowing anything about one another. The thing about being surrounded with politeness and composed self-confidence is it makes you want to mirror it; I wanted to be a grown-up gay like them, not the tangled mess of self-pitying introspection I felt when wandering around trying to find a frog-themed guest house.

Going round the table everyone introduced themselves: the artist wearing a brightly coloured scarf; the financier in his mid-fifties with his boyfriend in his early twenties, who'd just got back from a wine-tasting course (paid for by the older boyfriend) and perused the wine list at great length; and an older man wearing a blazer was sitting with his partner, a shorter, frail man who seemed too timid to say anything. They both seemed content in their shyness, like they would happily sit on their own saying nothing, which at first seemed very sad, then seemed actually fantastic. Not wanting to make them feel left out, I decided to start a conversation. 'What brings you both aboard?'

'Well,' said the man quietly in his gravelly and very wise voice, 'Jerry and I are from Maine—'

'I've worked as a drag queen my whole life!' piped up the frail Jerry out of nowhere and then slumped back into his quietness. The taller man continued.

'. . . and we just got married. We were the first people to do this in our community after the law changed. We did it at our church, and we didn't know who would come, but when we stepped outside, one hundred and fifty people from our local community were there – of their own freewill. We didn't know to expect that – we aren't very outgoing people, so this gesture from the community,' he continued with his deep, noble voice, 'was a real surprise.'

'So this is your honeymoon?!'

He laughed. 'Yes, I suppose it is, though at our age it feels a little beyond that. We just wanted to see something of the world.'

When I got back to the UK, I remember telling gay friends of mine about this cruise and comparing it to non-gay 'normal' cruises, and I was met with a very solemn rebuke and arched eyebrows. 'Er, being gay *is* normal!' they said with a quickness that suggested they spent their whole life ready to pounce on slip-ups – the sort of person who puts a camera on their bike helmet or who volunteered as an air-raid warden during the war.

These friends were, of course, correct, but in my limited experience at this point, I'd never had the luxury of being surrounded by people who were gay like me. It wasn't *ab*-normal, per se – it was *extra*-ordinary, and being extra is seldom a bad thing. It was wonderful to see people holding hands with people of the same sex without having to look over their shoulder to see if anyone was about to shout at them or worse. To see older gay people in love, who worked as drag queens and financiers and who languorously perused wine lists without fearing someone would throw a cucumber at them, was a sight far removed from the 'normal' I'd experienced on land. I didn't know a world like this could exist. 'Normal' is not always something to aspire to.

After dinner was the first of the fancy-dress parties. No wonder people were boarding with so many bags – they were packed full of the outfits for these daily extravagant parties. The combination of everyone being gay *and* mostly American meant that this truly was a no-holds-barred extravaganza. Themed around 'the ancient world', people created their own chariot to be Alexander the Great, or looked more like Cleopatra than she did with long-suffering partners stood at their side, dressed as the pyramids of Giza, bruised from getting their corners caught on the door frames.

'There you are!' said a drag queen dressed as a 1950s American housewife, complete with gingham apron and the biggest hair I had ever seen. I immediately recognised her – Dixie Longate! Dixie has made a career out of hosting drag Tupperware parties with upbeat inspirational finales. 'I've been looking for you – I'm just so glad you could make it!' she said in her broad American accent, her eyes sparkling in the evening sun.

'So, it was you who got me this gig?'

'Of course – I knew you'd be perfect for it. I told them they *had* to book you! Now, come on, let's get a tequila.'

Kris – sometimes known as Dixie – and I had met some months before doing a gig together, and we'd had such a great time chatting, I guess Kris had been generous enough to recommend me to the cruise organisers in Florida. This is why you must never be unkind to a drag queen; they are capable of more kindness than you could ever realise – why do you think they have to be so bitchy?

A tequila, lime and soda is a slow drink I recommend because it tastes so horrible you have to drink it very slowly. While the sun set over the funnel and I tried not to gag on my miserable beverage choice, Kris and I chatted about how to approach performing among this fun palace of swirly carpets and brassy handrails, where everyone is already a standout character. I am very grateful to anyone kind enough to recommend me for a gig, but then I always worry I'll let them down. Kris had put his own permed reputation on the line to recommend me, so I knew I had to do my best.

'You guys, this is Tom! He's the guy I was telling you about,' said Kris, announcing me to his assembled group of friends eating chips in the bright lights of the twenty-four-hour buffet.

'Oh, hello! Great to meet you guys!' This American confidence was really rubbing off on me; I was getting much better at announcing myself to groups of people – I could never imagine myself doing this in Bromley. I think I might have tried it on the first day of secondary school, but people looked the other way and laughed because it was deemed too flamboyant and too confident. This was different. It was time to get back to being that briefly confident child – the one who was just being himself but found the world didn't like it. To my delight, this group of gays and their friends responded.

'Hi, Tom!' they each said, smiling and seeming genuinely pleased to meet me. I met piano players, singers, drag queens, their friends, partners and all the guest entertainers aboard for this trip. 'Welcome to French Fry O'Clock!' said one of the piano players, offering me some of his chips.

'Hi, I'm Maria,' said another one of the singer-cum-piano players, 'and this is my husband, Jake!'

'Hi, I'm Jake!' said Maria's husband in an enthusiastic voice. His immaculately gelled hair, tight jeans and crop top meant I was more than a little surprised that he was married to a woman, but I wasn't on board to judge. 'We're going to watch Maria perform shortly,' rasped Jake with a tone that you knew meant, '. . . and you will come and watch.' Jake continued, 'It's going to be simply fantastic! I've been watching the rehearsals and her rendition of "Defying Gravity" – well, it is superb!'

'Oh my God, I love you,' said Maria, laughing and leaning in to kiss Jake on the lips. I stared at them for too long, intrigued by their set-up.

One of the drag queens quietly saw me looking and rolled their eyes as if to say, 'Yeah, they are an unusual couple, aren't they?'

Out of nowhere, Maria started singing the opening note of 'Defying Gravity' for no reason. Everyone instinctively went quiet, knowing that it was easier to go with the flow than fight against this tidal wave of musical theatre. Jake beamed as he looked on proudly; doe-eyed, he held his chin in his hands to watch another stellar performance from his musical-loving wife. Then he was distracted – irritated. 'What was that?' his face said as he turned in his chair to see a group of three men at the table behind him, innocently continuing their conversation and their fries, not realising they were supposed to be enjoying 'the performance of a lifetime'!

Unable to bear it a moment longer, Jake launched himself to his feet and marched over with his finger on his lips to tell them to be quiet immediately because his wife was performing. He then stood next to their table with his arms folded, eyes darting to anyone who even moved, to make sure no one dared interrupt again. Everyone looked terrified. A confused cruise member tried to make his way to the dessert station but turned back on seeing Jake (at every point in my life I always seem to be near some sort of dessert station). Maria reached her punishing crescendo, basking in the warm glow of the twenty-four-hour-buffet heater lamps and held her position, waiting for applause. The ensnared audience eventually put their fries down, resentfully, and under Jake's watchful glare, duly applauded.

Jake marched back over and leant in to kiss Maria again before she pulled back and slapped her knees. 'Oh, but you know what I want to see? Deck 13!'

'Oh yes – you must!' said everyone, glad to get out of there before she suggested an encore.

'What's Deck 13?' I asked.

'It's the Dick Deck,' responded Maria. 'You should come!'

Jake was already halfway up the stairs.

'Let's all go!' cried one of the drag queens, slamming down their plate of French fries.

'What do they mean the "dick deck"?' I asked Kris quietly as we all rose to leave.

'Oh, it's where they have the nude sunbathing in the day and some people seem to sneak up there to have sex when the sun goes down.'

Arriving in the quiet darkness of this deck at the back of the ship behind the funnel (not a euphemism), Maria exclaimed – 'I want to see the fucking! Where's all the fucking?'

Our motley crew of drag queens, musicians and stand-up comedians – like Dorothy and her friends apprehended by the Wicked Witch of the West – we rounded the corner to see nothing at all except in the darkness an occasional corner of flesh catching the moonlight. At one point, I thought I could see about twelve people, but Kris told me it was probably just a reflection in the brassy fittings and glass panels. I'd never seen anything like it – it didn't happen in *Queer As Folk*. It certainly didn't happen in *Titanic* either (though it would certainly explain why the women and children were in the lifeboats first – the men were clearly otherwise engaged).

'Oh, isn't it disgusting how some people behave?' said Jake, suddenly priggish. He seemed ridiculous, and then I realised I was just seeing a version of myself in him – that had been me at one time. Looking in from the outside, it seemed like such a waste of energy to be critical of anyone just doing their thing.

'Hush your mouth!' decried Maria. 'They're consenting adults having a good time. What difference does it make to you?' With the sound of Maria's booming off-Broadway voice, the heads attached to this writhing flesh suddenly turned.

'Is there a woman here?!' they could be heard whispering to each other, exhausted from their endeavours.

I suppose it isn't beyond the realm of possibility that we may have ruined the moment. Despite Maria's protestations – 'Don't stop – I love it!' – it was too late, and the men scattered. Maria really did have a type.

The next day, the sunshine blazed on our floating gay paradise, and so I took myself off to the swimming pool deck. I had never seen such confidence; American gays are world leaders in unapologetic living. Guys in the skinniest swimming trunks with sculpted, muscled bodies and men in their sixties and seventies with defined pecs and muscled butts sat next to guys with normal bodies, everyone relaxed and happy to be themselves. All of them just hanging out (not literally) in Jacuzzis, like different-sized chips frying in a pan. I cowered at the back with my pasty skin and swim shorts from Marks and Spencer.

'Oh, implants!' blurted out Kris, looking down at my flat chest and M&S swim shorts. 'They've all got implants! You can get implants wherever you want: chest, six pack, ass! Men in their eighties look like they've got the ass of their lives!' Ahh . . . It all made sense and I went back to feeling comfortable and not intimidated. I really loved being part of this poolside community, where I didn't feel like an outsider.

That night, waiting for our show to begin, I could feel the combination of stomach acid and heart palpitations that accompany any unfamiliar gig. By this time, I really liked everyone I'd met and I was having a wonderful time, so I felt all the more that I wanted to do my best for them. A challenge of stand-up is that you have to work hard and put your heart and soul into it, but when you're on the stage, you have to look like you're totally relaxed, like you were just walking past a theatre and thought to yourself, *Yeah I guess I could mooch in and say a few random things which happen to be insightful, truthful and, most of all, funny.*

The act before me seemed born to it! Walking out on stage, he loved being there and the audience loved watching him – snappy one-liners and tales about Deck 13 that the audience lapped up. This is the moment I usually want to run away, convinced that I can't ever be as confident as they are.

Waiting in the wings – knowing Kris was there to support me but in equal measure knowing I couldn't let him down – I was dreading how the audience would respond to my self-effacing, apologetic delivery. American stand-up audiences, unlike those in the UK, almost don't understand self-doubt – if you doubt yourself, why are you on stage? They love seeing people full of life – full of exuberance – alive to everything around them. If you seem insecure, they often feel it's a problem that needs to be fixed. The world I knew, growing up in the UK, felt to me like a place where I had to be the opposite, apologising for myself for being different, being gay, having the audacity to stand on stage – even being alive!

My name was called. I had to walk out there and deliver a confident version of myself. Maybe it would convince them – maybe it would even convince me – that I had a right to be there. Yet again, I did what Dad had taught me and walked out like I knew where I was going, that I could put up a fight if I needed to and I had money in my socks. I didn't walk into a chair, and I definitely didn't have to hold on to any bread rolls. 'Hey, are you having a good time?!' I said boldly.

'Yeah!' They shouted back (if you ask an American how

they are, they'll always reply enthusiastically and affirmatively). Positivity, while it can seem insincere or exhausting to British people, does have a habit of increasing the more it's bounced back and forth. I was feeling good – I was pushing almost to feeling confident – and I liked it. I liked making big gestures with my hands, using the whole stage to act out a story and doing exaggerated silly voices. It was in a way I'd never felt able to do before, and the audience liked it! I increased my delivery pace – they liked it even more. I put in a few jokes that felt like I was trying to be Joan Rivers: 'Hey, I was so drunk last night my cabin stood still!' I started telling stories – new stories I'd never told on stage about online-dating apps and the problem with campaigning for gay equality ('Why would we want equality when we can be better?') The American audience clapped. I didn't need to explain myself when everyone there had lived a similar experience. I spied the older couple on their honeymoon laughing and clapping along too.

'Was that OK?' I asked Kris afterwards, as I brushed past him in the shadow of a backstage curtain.

'You killed it!'

My heart sank before I remembered that killing it is a good thing.

Kris went on as Dixie Longate to also 'kill it', throwing Tupperware out into the audience and finishing with a rousing call to action: 'Live your life! Be the person you want to be – if it's what you want to do, get out there and shot-put a twink into the swimming pool.' The audience gave a standing ovation.

Relaxing on the top deck with Kris afterwards, I was relieved that I had done it without panicking and running into a life-boat and rowing back to England (I don't have the upper-body strength to pull myself out of a swimming pool, never mind row through the Strait of Gibraltar – whoever he is). The other performers came to join us, and we drank more and talked about the gigs of the evening. Jake was showing no signs of getting cold despite wearing very skimpy swimming trunks with a lace-up fly. He suggested, in celebration, that we all get in the hot tub. 'But we're not in our trunks!' I said peevishly.

'Oh you Brits are so uptight!' said Maria, slinking off the shoulder straps of her sequined stage dress. 'We'll just wear our underwear.' Suddenly, we were all there, squashed into this hot tub, laughing. Down the steps on the lower part of the deck, that night's costume party had segued into what happened every night – a DJ appeared and leather-clad bears came out to dance while a light show lit up the sky. With the pounding beats pulsating through the darkness along with laser beams high above us, it was as though we were on some big futuristic gay warship, pootling around the sedate ports of the Mediterranean.

I remembered when I was young, sat on that bar stool in Bromley eating Mini Cheddars, and now here I was surrounded by sea, marooned on an island of gays like the man had wanted to 'stick us all on'. Looking around me, it wasn't too bad at all.

9½

Driving

Looking back on these pages, it's almost as though I enjoy living my life with the handbrake on; I'm just about able to go at full speed, but something is holding me back, and there's smoke coming from under my bonnet and also a smell of burnt rubber in the air. You might think that wearing a bonnet at all is what has been holding me back, but I beg to differ; it turned out it was because I hadn't learnt to drive. So I decided to include here an ode to me passing my test.

It didn't seem a good idea to learn at seventeen when other people in my year learnt as it didn't suit me. I felt what suited me was learning how to play the piano and how to make frangipane. However, at thirty-two, I realised it was high time I started living life like other people did.

Another reason for learning to drive was that I had been booked to go on a tour that would mean I'd have to travel to places all around the UK, and I didn't feel like it was a good look for the evening's performer to be running out of the theatre and across town to get the last train home. As it turned out, I don't know how impressed the audience at the Hen and Chickens in Bristol were when queuing to go into the theatre, they were treated to a pre-show of me trying to parallel park by the front door for twenty minutes. Hot with frustration and rage and almost crying, I imagine they might well have questioned just how much fun was ahead of them from their entertainer.

Never having owned my own car, I got into the habit of hiring them, which was fun until I arrived at the rental depot and was told that because it was such a busy weekend, they'd run out of cars and so they'd allocated me a lorry – it wasn't a huge lorry but it was definitely a large van, and I had to go up some steps to get into the driver's seat. Luckily, as I was about to sign the carbon-printed docket, a man came in to tell them his van was too small.

Delighted, my ears pricked up and I slammed the biro on the clipboard and told him, 'Fear not! Do not worry – you can swap with me!' I think he was confused as to why such a flamboyant person was hiring any kind of truck in the first place, but he was pleased to make the swap and so I ended up in a smaller van, like the sort owned by a plumber, but one who didn't wear overalls. I still had enough space in the back that my suit carrier and holdall were flung from side to side as I turned corners – like Poor Joyce and I on that flume all those years ago.

The wonderful thing about being the driver of a white van is that everyone already assumes you're a bad driver, so they get out of your way and you barely have to worry about indicating because other drivers know you might change lanes at any moment. It was a real weight off my mind to know I had one less thing to do. However, I very quickly learnt about blind spots when I was on the motorway in the middle lane and realised I should be in the left-hand one. So, I checked my mirrors, indicated and went to manoeuvre, only to be beeped at very impolitely by the four-wheel drive Toyota I had, inadvertently, nearly pushed off the road.

I had also assumed that I'd attract a lot of road rage; I'm just the type and as it turned out, I wasn't wrong. The problem is, I still don't deal with confrontation very well – a man was once so abrupt to me at Orpington train station because I didn't understand about advanced open return tickets that I burst into tears. The people behind me in the queue were very alarmed. Dad made me phone the railway company to complain. The lady on the phone was very apologetic.

On the road, people can be so unforgiving, not realising how sensitive I am or that I might not know my way around their local roundabout, so naturally have to slow down to read all of the signposts – if everyone knew where they were going, they wouldn't have bothered putting the signs up in the first place. I wish instead of a bibber (I'm not sure if it's a bibber or a beeper or a horn), I could press a button and a loud voice could just say, 'I'm not from round here!' or, 'This is my first time on your roundabout and each arrow sign has a *lot* of places listed underneath it!' Maybe it could also shout something like, 'Sorry,' which feels like it would make the roads a much nicer place to be.

On single-lane country roads, drivers can be obnoxious as I found when I came face to face with one who refused to go back and expected me to reverse along the twisting lanes, which are stressful enough when facing forward never mind when going backwards and in the dark. What was in the Highway Code that meant they didn't have to reverse I don't know, but there was no time to ask as we both remained behind our windscreens. My friend Suzi was with me on that trip. It had taken us, by which I mean me, eight hours to get to Devon, mainly because I didn't go above second gear. We just stayed there in that lane, in a stand-off, face to face with the obnoxious van. It wasn't out of aggression that we didn't move, but because I couldn't get the car to go in reverse.

After that, trying to find our hotel along the winding roads, the satnav told me to take the next left and it turned out to be the driveway into someone's house – a dark and spooky house covered in ivy and no life there at all really, until suddenly a dog barked viciously, lights came on and a very aggressive man appeared. Suzi and I both screamed, convinced that we were going to be chased by a farmer who would inevitably kill us. We sped off and that was the night I learnt to go into third gear.

It's hard to believe, but I passed first time, after two practice tests. Before passing my last test, I'd managed to be fairly fast and loose with my driving instructors, who were either a bit blokey or who didn't have the right spark to complement my frankly quite needy demeanour. In learning to drive, I realised I needed an instructor who would sit next to me and constantly reassure me that I was doing fantastically and that I was probably the best driver they'd ever had the pleasure of teaching. Although if instructors had done that with me, I imagine we would have smashed into the central reservation of an A-road and my perfectly protected ego wouldn't have been any help at all.

Eventually, I stumbled upon the perfect teacher for me. I was doing gigs in Dundee on the east coast of Scotland and telling a story about how bad I was at driving. Afterwards I received a message from Claire in the audience telling me her cousin was a driving instructor in a place called Sidcup and was that near to me? Sidcup is the next town across from where I live. Simon arrived in a brightly coloured Hawaiian shirt and immediately knew how to be no nonsense in a way that shut me up but also wasn't afraid to say, 'You're a great driver.' Followed by, 'Watch out for that old woman!' As with so many things, it was a balancing act.

In addition to Simon, I knew I had to enlist extra help to boost my confidence with things like three-point turns and that one where you have to reverse around a corner. The idea of making people learn what must surely be the most dangerous thing imaginable was always a recipe for disaster. If you've turned a corner and you've made a mistake, it makes absolutely no sense to stop right there at said junction, and then drive back into the road you've just left, backwards. As far as I could tell from the lessons, examiners were looking for some sort of French clown mime act to demonstrate that you were looking over both shoulders all the time and going through a series of expressions from happy to surprised to downright sad, which I imagine would have to include tears in order for them to pass you. I understand that the DVLA has now removed this from the driving test – perhaps they'd had enough of all the clowning.

Nevertheless, I knew I had to get competent at it to pass the test, so I enlisted the help of my dad. My dad is an advanced driver and for most of my life worked as a coach driver. Coach drivers don't get the respect they deserve, carrying large numbers of people in huge unwieldy vehicles, often in the cramped conditions of the city where other drivers are impatient and not fond of the rules. Dad does have a certain way about him that doesn't always make him the most patient either. For example, he will often end telephone conversations by saying, 'I'm bored of you now!' which, while efficient, can sometimes seem a little abrupt. Similarly, as a coach driver, the team would often celebrate birthdays by passing a card around for everyone to sign. Instead of the usual *Happy Birthday, Lots of Love* . . . (though to be honest, how many colleagues have that much love for one another anyway) my dad would take to writing, *Shove It!,* and in a way I think they respected him more.

I asked Dad to accompany me for a practice run in the local Sainsbury's car park. On previous driving rehearsal expeditions, I found that Dad was very patient with me and on one occasion we even made it to Bluewater – the beloved out-of-town shopping centre frequented by people in South East London. It felt great to be out in Mum and Dad's Ford Fiesta Finesse, which was maroon – a colour that goes with nothing – had moss on the windows and brakes that squeaked, but I felt comfortable in it, mainly because it was so old it didn't matter if I scratched it on a width restriction. In fact, doing so might have removed some of the moss.

However, on this particular Sunday afternoon I noticed a distinct tonal shift. It wasn't his fault; he'd been working all week and now he was being dragged out by me to engage in highly dangerous manoeuvres for which I was still under-qualified. Like a clichéd character in a movie, I think I wanted to impress my dad and show him the new skills I'd been learning, despite having failed two practice tests already. I guess I wanted him to see that I'd been working hard at this new talent, and maybe, on some level, wanted him to see me as one day being as good a driver as he is. Maybe people might even ask *me* for a lift at some point.

I just needed to try to reverse into a parking space without anyone advising me, to show my dad and myself if I could do it without any help. The trouble is that people who accompany you when you're practising can do these things without thinking so they can't remember what it's like to be learning from scratch and they can't help but tell you what to do. This may also be connected to them fearing for their life.

'I'm only trying to help you. I just want to make sure you get it right,' said Dad, which was frustrating because I was annoyed at him for not letting me do it on my own but now felt guilty because he was clearly doing his best to look out for me. My plan to impress him had already fallen apart and instead we were bickering in a car park, which was very unlike a movie.

I knew it was time to head home when Dad started using my name, which, in a way, is the most damning of all chastisements: 'Tom! Watch out for that old woman! Tom!' – those old women seemed to be everywhere.

Leaving the car park and turning onto the high street, we arrived at some traffic lights. They were amber, so I stopped and waited for them to turn red. Dad seemed to be breathing a lot heavier, sighing even. The lights turned from red to amber to green and I went to move off and yet frustratingly, I stalled the engine. I turned the ignition to restart the car, but by this point the lights had gone back to red. Behind us, a white BMW pulled up. The lights turned to green and I prepared to drive away but, again, I stalled the engine. Dad muttered, 'Tom . . .' which only compounded my stress. 'Just stop panicking,' Dad advised, which is the most useless advice ever because that's not how feelings work. It's like if you're feeling nervous before making a speech and you get advised, 'Oh, don't be nervous!' as though you'd reply, 'Oh, thanks very much! I hadn't thought of it like that!'

Then to make matters even worse, as my heart raced and my hands got sweaty as they gripped the wheel so tight I could feel my knuckles cramp, the BMW driver bibbed their bibber (honked their horn sounds too rude). My dad, full of his 'shove-it' attitude and, on reflection, protective instinct over me, rather than placating the situation, turned round and gave them the middle finger at which point, furious, they seemed to lean directly on their bibber (actually horn would seem more apt here), causing the whole street to turn round and notice. After all of this, the lights had, of course, turned back to red.

Waiting now, in the din of the BMW's permanent bibbing, I was elated when the lights eventually turned to green. I managed to get the car going and swiftly moved off, just as the lights were going back to red. I moved so fast I didn't know if there was anyone on the crossing or anything – Dad didn't mention that old woman again though, so I assumed it was OK.

The BMW roared up behind us, overtook and then someone shouted out of the passenger window, 'You fucking c★★ts!' I was so shocked – hurt, even – I turned into some sort of Victorian school girl.

'Dad! But why? Oh why, oh why would someone speak to us like that?!'

My dad swiftly responded, 'Because they're slags! They're scum! Tell them to fuck off!'

'I can't tell them to fuck off – it doesn't sound right in my accent!'

'Do something right for once in your life!'

I knew I had to do it so I wound down the window, manually, because the car was that old, and shouted, 'Fuck! Off?' which sounded ridiculous because I said it so posh. Besides, the BMW was way out in front of us.

Now we were behind them. 'Now flash your lights at them!' said Dad.

I knew Dad was trying to make me tough and make me realise I was able to handle these situations, both on the road and in the wider world, but I just couldn't. I felt frustrated that maybe I was letting him down.

I had never been taught about flashing lights – my driving lessons had all been during the day and even if I had been told, I probably would have been too busy being needy and demanding more reassurances that I was both a good driver and also a good person. I thought I was flashing the lights, but I got confused – it was so stressful – and ended up turning the windscreen wipers on to full blast. I'd done it with real venom too so it went to max speed – it wasn't just one graceful wipe of the wipers and then back again, instead, the wipers speedily zoomed across the windscreen, like frantic, manic dancers in the musical *42nd Street* or the legs of The Rockettes doing their high kicks at Radio City Music Hall. The ridiculous high camp of their movement mocked my previous attempt to appear tough.

The water sprayed over the car, and cast jets of soapy water high above us, making us feel like we were in a Bromley version of the Bellagio fountains in Las Vegas. If the BMW driver had deigned to look back, they would have seen a ridiculous one-car gay-pride parade trying to pursue them aggressively, the driver flustered and out of control while he tried to impress his dad.

We drove home in silence, and when I pulled up in front of the house, I realised two things: it didn't matter if I got it wrong, because my dad was still looking out for me, and also that I'd kept stalling at the traffic lights because I'd literally been driving with the handbrake on.

In my final test, the examiner was at one point scrabbling at the door. It was as we were leaving a roundabout, and on seeing her do so, I immediately exclaimed, 'Oh God, I've done it wrong, haven't I? I've failed, haven't I? Let's go back to the base.'

All six foot two of Simon the driving instructor was squashed into the back seat, his Hawaiian shirt blinding me. He started to laugh. 'No, no!' exclaimed the examiner 'It's just that I asked you to take the fifth exit off the roundabout and you've taken the fourth exit.'

'I've done it wrong then – I've failed, haven't I?'

'No, no – we can't fail you for not being able to count.'

Somehow I passed the test. I was delighted and couldn't quite believe it. It was all worth it, less for the ability to drive, which I would always find terrifying, but more for when I got home to finally tell Mum and Dad. The initial look of pride quickly fading from their faces as it dawned on them that I would now be allowed on the road on my own.

IO

Standing

On the day I was due to perform my show at the London Palladium, I woke up in Leeds. I was on tour. Touring is fun because you get to go to so many places you didn't know existed – Ullapool has a food van selling fish that was once visited by Mary Berry, and Stockport has a museum all about hats. The only thing that makes touring difficult is sleeping. Hotels that aren't very nice aren't comfortable for good sleep, while hotels that are too nice keep you awake because it feels like such a waste to be somewhere beautiful and be unconscious for the whole experience.

I woke up too early out of excitement because that night's show felt like an especially big deal, and it was being filmed. I'd not had any kind of multi-date tour before, though by this point I had been a stand-up for nearly fourteen years. So many times, I had been on the cusp of giving up comedy altogether, even though I had scraped a living doing gigs in rooms above pubs and in comedy clubs; I just didn't know if people would ever understand what I was talking about.

In Edinburgh two years before, I had found myself in a performance space that was far too big for me. I could only really fill the smallest rooms, and even then the fifty seats would be mostly empty until the weekends. The room I was allocated was supposed to be a gentle increase to seventy-five seats, but when I got there, it was clearly a room for *one hundred* and seventy-five. It was much bigger than I could ever fill, and since it was right over the other side of the city from the rest of the festival and it seemed to rain every day, when audiences did get there they sat confused, damp and vaguely annoyed.

When they sat down, they were so massively spaced out in this huge room (which was really designed for wedding banquets and corporate AGMs) that even if they did feel like laughing, they were too self-conscious to make a sound. A very strict technical manager would turn off the microphone and put the strip lights on if I overran, even if we'd been delayed by earlier shows. The whole thing felt like a nightmare and there was no one to speak to about it, and I was exhausted and ready to go back and work in a normal job and think about getting some hanging baskets.

As is the case with so many unenjoyable incidents, they make you want to run away and you'll do anything to get out of them, but in retrospect you see they were very positive learning experiences. Small crowds in intimate spaces make you tough because you have to learn how to make everyone relax and feel confident that you know what you're doing – if you show them even the smallest crack in your armour, they'll be unable to laugh because they'll spend the whole time worrying about you. On one Saturday afternoon, thirty people came in from the Edinburgh drizzle, including a couple with a carrier bag full of beers, and the man, being drunk, repeated everything I said. A posh English man sitting in front of him turned round and proclaimed, 'Can you shut up, please? It's very rude!'

He was right, but it didn't make my job any easier – Scottish people really don't like being 'told off' by English people. 'Fuck you – he's just got back from working on the rigs. Can't he enjoy his-fucking-self?!' said his wife.

'Yeah, can't I——' said the drunk man (incoherently).

'Shut up, Brian!' his wife snapped back at him. In a large theatre full of people, it would be very easy to deal with this because the whole room would goad them to leave so they didn't disrupt the evening, but in a room of thirty, everyone was actually quite scared of them. Also, when the audience is unsure of how good the comedian will be, it crosses their mind that this disruption might be more entertaining than the show itself.

'Maybe you should leave?' shouted an Edinburgh accent from the other side of the massive room to the drunk pair.

'All right then – fuck yous!' said the drunk couple, stumbling out with their bag of beers and, as it turned out, Pringles (dinner *and* a show!). The posh man in front led a smug round of applause with his hands cupped above his head as he watched them go.

I had experienced dealing with different types of audience because my friend Sarah Millican had taken me on tour with her as her support act. Sarah is a kind, soothing voice who encouraged me, and made the stand-up world seem much friendlier. Being a support act means you perform before the main act in huge rooms to large crowds of people who have specifically come out to not see you. You learn very quickly how to hold your nerve, how to fake confidence and how to respond quickly to anything unexpected. The drunks interrupting my Edinburgh show were just an extension of this. I knew I had to maintain my confidence and not let the audience see my nervousness.

However, when you're playing to a small crowd and trying to get people to see the world from your perspective for a long time and no one knows who you are, you start to question what the hell you're doing. Shamefully, it feels like an imposition that you've written a show about your experiences and then have the audacity to turn up in another city and ask people to pay to come and see it (though truth be told, the Edinburgh Fringe ticket money seldom makes its way to the performer – accommodation and the cost of hiring the venue take all of that and more from most comedians). Standing there, you can feel like a child who's asked their parents and parents' friends to sit in rows while you jump out from behind the curtains in the lounge, knowing that this is how a play starts, but not realising you have to have something to actually perform.

After the show, I made a habit of shaking people's hands to say thank you for coming. One day, a short older man, shaking my hand, pulled me warmly towards him and gently whispered in my ear, 'That was the longest hour of my life.' Having taken onboard all the advice I'd been given over the years about the importance of appearing tough and robust and not showing any crack in my armour, I abruptly burst into tears. I still had a long way to go before I stopped caring what people thought.

Thanks to the encouragement of friends I lived with in Edinburgh – Amy Annette, Nish Kumar, James Acaster, Josh Widdicombe, Rose Hanson, Stu and Sarski Goldsmith, Joel Dommett and Steve Dunne and, as ever, Suzi Ruffell (long list, eh? Did I mention Edinburgh flats are expensive during the festival?) I kept going and kept laughing in the downtime we had around our shows. It reminded me that despite all the drama, comedy is just a bit of a laugh.

Also the management company Off the Kerb had come to see me, brought by Suzi and Josh. Flo Howard took me out for lunch but I didn't really know why – in my mind perhaps she felt sorry for me. To my surprise, she offered me representation, and I was truly blown away. Suddenly I was part of Flo's stable of clients and also the wider Off the Kerb family – the management company who developed the careers of Alan Carr, Michael McIntyre, Jonathan Ross, Kevin Bridges and (the most generous and kind person I've ever shared a television set with . . .) Jo Brand. I'd been terrified of them before because they were always so professional and so well regarded in the industry and I was just an oddball trying to tell anecdotes in a wedding venue in Edinburgh.

However, they were totally behind me from the get-go and I felt invincible – with encouragement and support, human beings can help one another do anything. Despite still living at home and still carrying my familiar old insecurities, things were starting to shift. Bookings for panel shows were starting to come in – *Cats Does Countdown* invited me to be in Dictionary Corner, *Bake Off*'s *An Extra Slice* had me on as a guest and *The John Bishop Show* asked if I'd like to do stand-up on their Christmas special. This involved appearing with Kylie Minogue for the finale, where the whole cast had to go on stage to sing 'Last Christmas' with Olly Murs. She stood next to me in the wings and I told her I'd been teased at school because I couldn't sing. She reassured me by saying, 'Don't worry, just stick your finger in one ear and look like you're harmonising – that's what a globally famous *chanteuse* does.' If only I'd been taught this at school.

Flo taking me on as a client was a real turning point. To give you an idea of what Flo is like, while being wheeled into labour for the birth of her first child, she found out that the midwife's favourite comics just so happened to be me and my friend Suzi Ruffell and then *sorted tickets for the midwife* for our forthcoming show. She is truly the most hard-working person I know, as well as the kindest, and it is because of her taking me under her wing that I started to feel like I didn't have to worry about what people thought, as long as Flo was on my side I'd be all right.

It was Flo, alongside Kerb's tour-booking guru and gentle giant (as well as managing director and ardent Radio 4 listener) Joe Norris, who booked my first tour of thirty venues. I drove myself to the first one, and while being nervous, I was also exhausted. Mainly because my cautious driving style meant I had been on the road all day and arrived moments before the start of the show. Screeching the car to a halt on the theatre's forecourt, I ran onto stage immediately to start performing in Southport, breathless like I was in *Challenge Anneka* or something. The next day, I drove myself to Carlisle and started to realise I loved touring – the gig was sold out and I even enjoyed getting myself from place to place under my own steam and meeting all the wonderful people who kindly came to see me!

The show I was touring was the fruition of all the gigs in comedy clubs and bars, the anguish over whether or not the audience would like me, the tweaks to material that only came from doing it over and over; gigs I wouldn't have been able to do in the first place if it wasn't for the lifts from my dad to the station. I loved performing it, but what I also loved was when I got to talk to the people in the audience – it turns out that when you've got a microphone, people will tell you anything. I loved hearing about their lives, how they'd had an argument with their partner so taken their sister instead, how they'd got a pet parrot because he was better company than their husband, how they'd struggled to park their Ford Fiesta so had to leave every half an hour to feed the meter – I suddenly had all these friends and I'd never even met them before.

The tour was extended for a further sixty dates. A few nights at the Soho Theatre turned into two weeks at the Soho Theatre. I ended up doing 160 dates across the tour, and there were thoughts about doing the show at a larger London venue near the end of the run. Flo suggested the London Palladium – 'I feel like it's your spiritual home!'

I would never have dreamed of performing my show in a place like this – this was where Bruce Forsyth had performed *Sunday Night at The London Palladium* and had his ashes interred beneath the stage; Judy and Liza recorded a concert there; Philip Schofield had played Joseph there. Flo believed in me and the show sold out.

She was right about me feeling a connection to the place, notably my school summer-holiday project that I took great pride in completing at the end of Year 5. We had to do a poster about something we loved. Being an eccentric nine-year-old, rather than doing it about my holiday to Spain, I decided I would do mine about theatre and proudly entitled it The Thespian World! I basically copied out everything about the theatre I found in the programme for *Joseph and the Amazing Technicolor Dreamcoat*. Unfortunately, owing to some mis-spacing in my poster's bubble writing, there was a gap mid-word, so the poster's title looked like I'd written *THE THE SPIAN WORLD*, and everyone just thought I'd misspelled Spain and made a poster about a rather flamboyant and Technicolor holiday.

My other experience of the London Palladium had been when I performed at the Royal Variety Performance. The Duke and Duchess of Cambridge looked on from the royal box. It was a stressful experience not just because I was on straight after a truly lovely acrobatics group who I kept worrying would drop each other smack down onto the stage, but also because there had been a bomb scare just as we were getting ready to start the show. I got a phone call from my mum who had been en route to the theatre and was suddenly stampeded by police into H&M in Oxford Circus with Dad. 'Your dad's never been in here.' She sounded terrified. 'The trousers are too skinny for his thighs!' It dawned on me that this might be the last conversation I ever got to have with them.

The whole cast was suddenly told to make their way to the auditorium, those school fire drills finally coming in handy. I was with Torvill and Dean, Michael Ball, Joan Collins and the band of the Irish Guards, all of us sat beneath a very precarious chandelier in the stalls of the theatre. All I could think was, *If I die here, alongside all these famous faces, none of the headlines will ever even mention me.*

I only had one interaction with Joan Collins, who I walked past when we were eventually allowed to return to our dressing rooms. She was sitting down and I smiled at her to which she responded, haughtily, 'You've got something on your shoe.' I looked down and *somehow* I'd managed to get toilet roll stuck to my sole. How it got there, I don't know. Maybe it was thrown at me by one of the Irish Guards. I may never know. That was my one interaction with Joan Collins.

So, back to that morning in Leeds. I was due to do my own show for one night at the Palladium, filmed for television, stressful enough as it was, but there was worse to come. Waking up early, I thought it might actually be a better idea to sleep a bit longer and get an eleven thirty train to London. I didn't need to be at the theatre until three, so there was no rush – I'd only end up walking round the block as I had done at that first gig in Bethnal Green. I arrived at the station and waited calmly for the train and then suddenly an announcement: all trains going south were cancelled and 'passengers travelling to London are advised to take alternative routes', which basically meant trekking across the country to Manchester and changing.

I immediately chastised myself. *This is what happens when you rest and take an extra hour to sleep – you're so lazy! The train you* should *have got was running perfectly on time!*

I boarded the packed Manchester train with one cheek up against the window, my hand gripping my bag, which was wedged against someone's guitar, only to be told that the train was now only going halfway to Manchester and we'd all have to get off in the Peak District and wait for the next one. I felt sick and stressed and even more furious with myself for sleeping for too long. I wondered if I should get a cab. *Can you get Ubers from the Peak District to the London Palladium?* I wondered. *How long would that take? What would it cost?*

I changed trains in Manchester and, luckily, managed to get one of the last trains down to London which, due to the earlier cancellations, was packed with business people, hen parties and a drunk rugby team who kept sitting on my wheelie case. I had treated myself to a first-class ticket because you get a bigger seat and a biscuit – but this didn't provide much consolation with such a crowded service. The basket of shortbread appeared out of nowhere over a rugby player's ample shoulder as I cowered in the corner of the carriage by the luggage rack.

Rather than a sedate arrival early in the afternoon, I found myself dashing through crowds of Christmas shoppers who all seemed to walk too slowly, dawdling on escalators in the peak of the afternoon rush. My luggage got caught in the barriers of the Tube station; at the end of my tether, I pulled it through and set off the alarm. 'Oi! You could break it by yanking it like that!' said an irate London Underground worker.

If I'd been feeling more upbeat, I would have responded with a raised eyebrow but I was too stressed and in no mood for innuendo. 'I am late!' I hollered theatrically, 'For the London Palladium!'

As I got to the theatre with my wheelie suitcase, I glanced up to see my face above the entrance on the digital poster board. I had arrived! It was the culmination of everything I had been working towards, but, as is often the case in life, there was no time to dwell, just a stolen glance as I wheeled past. I was also conscious that people (probably from Bromley) would see that I was gazing romantically at a picture of my face and say, 'Look at him! Vain sod!'

Before I knew it, I was on the stage doing my sound check and taking in where the cameras would be. I was four hours late for the biggest day of my career, a day I'd been preparing for since the school project when I was nine. Nonetheless, regardless of the stress, I was there.

'Speak slowly and don't shout,' said Flo gently as I sat on the dressing-room floor polishing my shoes. She was right. When I'm nervous, I have a tendency to shout. It's a combination of trying to get the audience's attention, learnt in loud, drunken stand-up clubs, and a way of drowning out the voice in my head telling me I'm not good enough to be there.

While I was checking out how it felt to walk around the stage, what the lights would feel like and how my voice sounded on the sound system, Flo had taken a photo of me and posted it to her Instagram. *Dreams do come true.* It was so overwhelming to think that I was there at the end of a tour that had lasted eighteen months, having worked hard for fourteen years, and now, under Flo's steady guidance, we'd made it here. It was kind of too much to think about, so I tried to push it out of my head all together and did what I always do when I need to focus: I polished my shoes again.

Sat on the floor of Dressing Room 1 where Bruce Forsyth and Larry Grayson had got ready for their shows, I just concentrated my energy on putting the polish on and buffing it away to reveal shoes a bit shinier than they'd been before. I think I was desperate to make sure I didn't get toilet paper stuck to them again.

Friends had told me they'd be there, including my friend Lili (who'd flown in from New York especially), Liam Charles (with whom I co-host *Bake Off: The Professionals*), Rob Beckett (my great friend and schoolmate), Amy Annette and Nish Kumar (who I lived with during the Edinburgh Fringe), my friend Eleanor Thom, my dad's childhood friend Andy Norman and mum's friend Aunty Jilly. Her and her husband, Bruce, had even bought a box. Part of me still felt a terrible fear that I'd let them all down – how could I drag them here, to this huge venue? I just kept polishing my shoes.

When it was nearly time for the show to begin, Flo came in to tell me that we should head down to the stage. The backstage areas of theatres are seldom very glamorous and usually quite cramped and tend to be in the same style as when the theatre was built because no one bothers about modernising them. In arts centres built in the 1990s, they look like *The Brittas Empire*; if from the 1970s, they feel like the set of *Crossroads*.

At the Palladium, it's different because they make it nice for people like Joan Collins. They painted it all grey and for some reason put in lots of desks for chorus dancers to sit and do their make-up at. It's very swish, but with all the desks, it can look a bit like a call centre. There are also lots more people than a lot of theatres because it's such a huge venue and needs a lot of staff to make sure idiots like me don't take a wrong turn and end up like the Phantom of the Opera suspended from the chandelier. Flo and I stood in the darkness of the huge wings at the side of the stage, ropes seemed to be going in different directions to hold up all the curtains – curtains much bigger than my mum's tie-backs could ever hope to hold.

The theatre manager came to tell me that the house was almost ready – which sounds very formal but which basically means the drunks are nearly done with ordering booze at the bar. Finally, getting the all clear in his earpiece, he made a slight bow of his head, in courtly fashion, and said, 'Standing by.' I was a stand-up standing by.

The job of a stand-up means we often travel on our own, we walk out on the stage on our own, we perform on our own, and so it's up to us to walk out and do it. In that moment when the show is ready to start, we make the decision on our own to physically walk out there and get the job done. Despite the many times I'd wanted to run away, I never had.

Finally, with no announcement, I walked out on stage and the audience kindly applauded. We'd begun.

Walking out in a large venue is a strange feeling because you feel like you want to thank everyone for being there. I try to do this in any venue by acknowledging the various corners of the room. In a venue like the Palladium, you get a sore neck because the people in the top tier are so high above you. Apart from that, it's the same as the arts centre where I'd started the tour just outside Liverpool; it's the same as the tiny corner stage where I'd warmed up the show in Edinburgh. It's the same as the space between the window and the tied-back curtains where I'd insisted Mum and Dad watch me do a show that didn't exist when I was four. It's even the same as a school cabaret when I didn't know what I was doing, I just knew I wanted to be there.

It would have been too much for me to think about all of these things at once. And as a stand-up, you learn to bury your vulnerabilities in clubs where people shout you off the stage. At the end of the first half, I announced the interval and thought about how afterwards I'd like to get a cheeseburger from Five Guys next door.

During the interval, I sat in the dressing room, wondering how it was going and contemplated giving my shoes another polish. I thought they'd been laughing, but I couldn't be sure – Flo popped by to reassure me it was going well. The twenty-minute break was over before I knew it, and suddenly I was back on stage, and then, almost without realising, we were at the end of the show. I said some thank-yous and, since I had spent so much of the show doing impersonations of them, introduced the audience to two people who were watching. I gestured with my arm to the royal box where Prince William and Kate had sat at the Royal Variety Show. 'Ladies and gentlemen, I'd like to introduce you to my mum and dad!' It suddenly dawned on me how very exposed they were, perched on high with me talking about them in front of all these people.

I needn't have worried though as they were immediately on their feet proffering royal waves at the assembled crowd who gave them a rousing round of applause. I felt a huge surge of emotion and found myself blinking away tears as quickly as possible before the audience noticed. I realised I still worried about them, but given their stately response from the box, maybe they were ready to fend for themselves.

Finally, the tour was finished and after all this excitement, I needed a holiday. It can be difficult to switch off in our online age – emails and social-media messages come in at all times of the day and night. It's the first thing I check in the morning and the last thing I check before bed, and as someone who's self-employed, I always feel I might miss out on work. I get to do a job that's fun and joyful, and I get to meet so many wonderful people that I hope I repay the favour by working as hard as I can.

My friend Suzi Ruffell and I decided to go to New York for the celebration of WorldPride. Suzi and I have been friends since we both did a charity gig where we had to do stand-up after a drag queen had led the crowd in a singalong. It proved impossible because after two hundred drunk gay people have been introduced to the wonder of their own voices belting out in unison, the last thing they wanted to do was stop and listen to singular voices tell them about their perspective on their mum's kitchen. Suzi and I both had the same experience of dying in front of that audience, and we have been friends ever since.

We had started doing a podcast, *Like Minded Friends*, where we talk about our experiences of being gay and we've been thrilled that so many listeners are able to listen and enjoy and share our experiences of not always being able to live up to what people expect of us, amongst other things.

WorldPride is a Pride festival, held in a different city each time. New York hosted it in 2019 because it was the fiftieth anniversary of the Stonewall Riots. Pride is something I've supported since I first came out because it fosters a sense of belonging and brings people together in solidarity with the goal of advancing equality. I know a lot of people have felt like the name doesn't quite match how they intrinsically feel when so many experiences in life have hampered them feeling 'proud'. I know that for me, Pride slogans like 'Love is Love' while positive and true, have sometimes compounded my sense of not fitting in, I suppose, because I've never properly been in love.

However, I've come to learn that the concept of Pride is perhaps best seen as a goal or even as a verb and something we are all striving for on our personal journeys – to learn that we are all valid, important, and ultimately, enough – while we hopefully work towards achieving this for other people.

Pride, as a celebration of how far we've come, can be a lot of fun and you get to drink in the street, and strangers are nice and people smile at each other. It used to be a march, but now it's a parade and you're supposed to pre-register to be part of it which, while safety conscious, feels less fun if you have to be a spectator. Ever keen to do the opposite of what I'm supposed to do, one year I snuck past the officious marshals in high-vis vests and walked alongside a team of very snooty flight attendants who looked at me like I'd broken into business class from economy.

So, for our holiday, Suzi and I were making the trip to New York where *Attitude* magazine and Virgin Atlantic dedicated an entire flight to taking the LGBTQIA+ community over to WorldPride in New York. It even had the flight number VS69 (this was genuinely the call sign for international air traffic control). The bar was stocked with enough booze for three return trips to Las Vegas but was drunk dry within three hours of the eight-hour flight.

A drag queen DJ'd from the front, and we went and danced – sneaking into business class, but no one minded. Singers sang to us while walking up and down the aisles. It was a wild party, except for the straight family who booked the flight by accident. They took it with good grace but I think they found it difficult to order a club soda and respond to the classic 'Chicken or beef?' catering questions when Donna Summer was blasting out of the speaker system and a drag queen was gyrating against the bulkhead.

There were also families who wanted to take their children on their first Pride experiences and wanted to do it in style. Even to my cynical stand-up's heart, this did seem pretty lovely.

Arriving in New York, we all had to wait in line for the stern immigration staff. A number of our travel-mates had to be told, more than once, to stop singing show tunes. And to stop swaying. And to stand up. I'm sure they got it together in the end and they were allowed into America. In that state, I can't imagine they'd have been able to find their way home.

The whole trip was ridiculous fun. We went to a party at the top of the new World Trade Centre and we went to a piano bar and saw the pianist from the cruise ship. Unfortunately, I had to leave because Suzi said I was shouting out over the Broadway singers who had stopped by to belt out rousing numbers for the nice old gays sat at the bar (drinks are stronger in the US, everyone knows this). We went to the Metropolitan Museum of Art to look at an exhibition of camp – it was so much more joyous than my previous trip. ('Exhibition of

Camp' could be the name of my next tour show). We had cocktails on the roof, and one of us *may* have thrown up. It didn't matter.

And of course, Suzi and I went to watch the Pride parade and were amazed by the acrobatics of a passing group of LGBTQIA+ cheerleaders. They were fantastic and seemed much nicer than the snooty cabin crew I'd met in London. Yet I still had the nagging feeling that I wasn't doing it quite right. I wasn't upbeat and proud enough. I hadn't made a placard to hold and I wasn't part of some huge organisation – I was just there, still feeling like I was on the outside, still too awkward to jump in the pool.

After I'd asked for a photograph with some policemen and tried to flirt with them unsuccessfully, we turned off the main street where the parade was to get an ice cream. Walking away from the hub of the festivities, the loud music, the masses of people, I began to realise it's OK to not be in the middle of proceedings all the time. Present in the moment and present in yourself is enough. So often we feel we're not enough, that we should be somehow different – that we should offer more.

The truth is, everyone is an outsider somewhere, and that's OK.

What I love about stand-up is that it has the potential to include everyone – audiences hunger for new stories, people different to themselves, outsiders representing who they are and the view from where they stand. There are lots of theories about why we actually need laughter, but for me, it's about a primal instinct to connect with the person on stage. The comedian speaks about their experience and the audience feels the same way, remembers the same thing, experiences the same insecurities and they let out this spontaneous response to say,

'Yes, I am here too.' Performing stand-up, I've realised I've only improved when I've embraced my insecurities, my eccentricities and enjoyed telling my stories as an outsider, however awkward I might feel about it at first. Stand-up is about being confidently insecure.

I hope that anyone who can relate feels validated but also relieved that they too are allowed – and not just 'allowed', but empowered – to walk around on a stage and live their life with positivity and joy.

We all experience shame, a product of the moments in our past that make us frightened to live our lives to the full in the present. It hangs around our necks, making us feel less than the person next to us, but if we can drag it out into the open and see what it is and see how we all share in this human experience, maybe we can see that we're not so bad after all. I am proud of my show at the Palladium because I managed to be confident in my insecurities, knowing that everything was as it should be, that all my flaws were part of that moment and part of me.

The stand-up should stand up to be counted, should stand up for anyone who has been in the same situation. They stand up for being different, for being flawed, for being a human being and somehow, hopefully, we all leave the show feeling less alone in the world and maybe, just a little less ashamed.

Epilogue

In conclusion, I thought I should write a letter to my younger self to let him know how things turn out. So here it is:

August 2020

Dear Tom,

I write this to you, my sixteen-year-old self, with some news from your future thirty-seven-year-old self. I want to reassure you about a few things.

First, you'll be pleased to know that coming out doesn't prove to be such a cataclysmic moment for you. To be honest, the top hats and the love of Noël Coward mean that people have a pretty strong sense that you might be gay anyway.

You make friends who understand you and you get to do a job you love doing, though there are times when it's tough. The main thing I want to convey is don't worry. You panic about everything and you fear everyone but you don't need to – it's exhausting both for you and the people you come into contact with. I mean, do worry a bit – it's probably good to keep you motivated, and also if you didn't worry, you'd be a totally different person. Now I'm worrying about how this is going to be misconstrued. As you can tell, you always worry.

I think you worry about making mistakes and looking foolish and vulnerable. This is the shame you carry. You need to know if other people make you feel like this, it's their issue not yours and you'll come to think of them as the dreadful people that they truly are. You are allowed to make mistakes and try things and create things and make work of varying quality and get it all wrong and it's all OK because you're entitled to learn. That's part of being a human being.

The times you spend on your own and in your own head are important. Trusting that voice is sometimes useful to make you realise your own value and to keep things on your terms but don't forget it's OK to talk to people when you need to.

The world will change and while there is still a long way to go in terms of equality, gay people can now get married. Although this will make you envious of people who have managed to fall in love and do this, overall you will think it's a good thing.

The things that seem like such a big deal really aren't, and laughter will be the best way to minimise their impact and will help you connect to the people around you. Also, no one really cares about anything you do because they'll be much too preoccupied with their own lives. Try to remember this.

Finally, even though you are fearful of so much in the world and nervous about your place within it, know that there is more love out there than you know. There is kindness and generosity from people you meet at every turn. Don't be ashamed to love them all back.

Yours,

Tom

It felt very cathartic to write to my younger self like this. Imagine my surprise then to receive a response from my sixteen-year-old self. He writes:

August 1999

Dear Tom,

How nice of you take the time to write me, as you know I am very busy at the moment, so while this was a welcome break from my studies, it was also an unwelcome distraction. I cannot believe that it has taken you until the age of thirty-seven to write a book. This was something that should have been completed long before you even turned thirty – *what* have you been doing?

I also notice that you don't mention anything interesting about living arrangements – which leads me to conclude that you must still be living at Mum and Dad's? Jeez, I thought we'd be living in Monte Carlo by this point. Again, what on earth have you been doing with all this time? This is very disappointing news indeed.

Also the World Wide Web – is it a big deal like everyone says it will be?

I imagine that after writing the book you will have spent a long time looking inwards and thinking about the things big and small that happened. Just know that it's OK – even I know it's all exactly as it should be. The things which happen come along at the right time. Living with Mum and Dad isn't so bad. Remember, you don't have to explain yourself to anybody.

Now, if you'll excuse me, I have an appointment with a man about a top hat.

With love,

Tom

Acknowledgements

The first people I should say thank you to are my teachers and in particular my two A-Level English teachers, Ms Abbott and Ms Brown, who I hope are proud of my writing here. Ms Abbott taught me that it was OK to love Alan Bennett openly and that *Talking Heads* is brilliant even if no one else in the school seems to know what it is. Ms Abbott also opened the door to a whole new world of modern literature by getting us to read *The Buddha of Suburbia* by Hanif Kureishi and showed us that suburbia was worth writing about and that the everyday could be fantastic. Ms Brown taught us that television writing was part of literature as we studied Dennis Potter and *The Singing Detective,* and I was mesmerised by how creative you could be with the worlds you create on the page and on the screen.

I also had fantastic drama teachers including Ms Liles, Ms Polaszek and Ms Butcher (who told me about the National Youth Theatre) and music teachers Mrs Sowter, Ms Banerjee, Ms Werry (who introduced me to Noël Coward) and Mr Rollings. In other subjects, Ms Jamieson, Mrs Millar, Ms Wickens, Ms Wood and Ms Chandler, all of whom supported me in various ways throughout my eccentric teenage years in a world that often didn't feel very eccentric at all.

I'd also like to thank Sarah Millican, Jo Brand, Josh Widdicombe, Rob and Lou Beckett and Alan Carr for reading early copies of the book and for all their advice and support. Thanks to Alexa, Bri, Suzi and Alice for always being there and for reading segments along the way. I would not have been able to complete it without the guidance of Phil Jerrod and Eleanor Thom. Phil gave me the advice that people might be annoyed if you include them but they'll be furious if you leave them out, so I apologise wholeheartedly to the many people not mentioned in the book who have contributed to these stories in so many ways.

No book gets made without the patience and insight of an editor and publishing team, and I am very grateful to everyone at Hodder Studio including Izzy Everington, Rebecca Millar, Meryl Evans and especially my editor Myfanwy Moore.

Thanks Aemen Sukkar and everyone at Jiksaw for the jacket design and photo and for always being more encouraging than they needed to be.

Thanks to Jilly and Bruce and Miss Hammond for supporting me and understanding me before I knew myself, and thanks to the neighbours in Bromley, mum's friends for letting me listen in on their conversations, Jill for telling me to have a voice and Luke the boxer for keeping me calm.

Thanks as always to Flo Howard, Lily Morris, Katy Helps and the family at Off The Kerb for always having my back.

Lastly thanks to my family, my brother James, our four legged friend Bo and, as always, my mum and dad – I promise I'll move out soon and please may I have a lift?